THE TRUTH AND THEORIES

The Many Faces of Christopher Watts

CHERYLN CADLE

ISBN 978-1-961227-59-0 (paperback)
ISBN 978-1-961227-61-3 (hardcover)
ISBN 978-1-961227-60-6 (digital)

CC Press
cjcadle@hotmail.com
815-549-6439

Printed in the United States of America

Edited by: Michael Cadle

CONTENTS

INTRODUCTION

The purpose of my book is to bring the truth to help bring anyone to justice that is guilty. My hope is the Law Enforcement agencies will take another look into this case and bring justice for Shanann, Bella, Cece and Nico.

Quoting the Bible scripture: And he said, What hast thou done? the voice of thy brother's blood crieth unto me from the ground. (Genesis 4:10) KJV

This man, this monster, came into my life in January 2019. Just five short months after he had murdered his entire family. Everyone in the Christopher and Shanann Watts home was wiped out. Cruel for no reason—a senseless, crazy act of evilness was brought on, in my opinion, by his mistress, who gave him everything he thought he lacked. He was propelled by lust and sex, which fed his appetite, for an insatiable appetite for more. Christopher Watts has always said something controlled him that eerie morning of August 13, 2018. Was this true, or was this casting blame? Still today, he will say he does not completely recall everything that happened. I started to believe he didn't remember everything. Five years later, he still says that morning, or at least part of that morning, is unclear. How can an act of this level of evilness be excused by the perpetrator as not remembering? I would think you wouldn't be able to get it out of your head and mind. I would think it would haunt you daily. Guess what? It does haunt him every day and every night of his pathetic life. I believe Shanann's brother was hoping this would be Christopher's fate.

Why write this book? I'm sure there will be some, especially the media trolls, that will accuse me of only doing it for money. I'm sure

I will be accused of all sorts of things. However, because I am just like so many of you, I cannot get this case out of my mind. Also, I have found out several things I believe those who are so invested in this case need to know. It haunts me every day. It interferes with my sleep; it visits my dreams. I think of Shanann as a motivated, busy mom who was true to her family and was taken without warning. I'm sure no matter what she was going through with her marriage, it never entered her mind that Christopher could or would kill her and the girls. He told me once that one thing he feels so bad about is the last thing he said to Shanann: "I don't love you." She died hearing that, and that was as cruel as it gets.

Many have tried to blame Shanann for Christopher's outburst of evil. Shanann was strong-willed, determined, driven, and probably bossy. However, according to Christopher himself, he lacked the take-charge personality that a woman as strong as Shanann needed. With his personality, she had to be the strong one, but now people try to blame her for her murder. I cannot tell you how this angers me! This poor mother of three was not given any chance to defend herself. Her husband murdering her, I believe, came completely by surprise, and she must have died, not being able to grasp why he would do this. We do know she died not knowing her competition. What kind of coward would do that? This kind of coward.

People say every death has a purpose. I was told this repeatedly after my eighteen-year-old grandson's death. I have never figured out a reason for his death, nor can I figure out why Shanann, her unborn son, Bella, and Cece's death either. It makes no sense whatsoever. The only way I can think of it is untimely. We know God did not ordain Christopher to kill his family; it was done out of self-will and pure evilness from the monster that lives inside of him. Although you will see why I think his girlfriend played an integral role in the murders, this monster grew inside of him when he was a very young child; this is my belief and opinion.

Looking back, one of the darkest days in my life is the day I felt called to write about the Christopher Watts murders. I've had the wonderful opportunity to talk with many people worldwide because of my book, *The Murders of Christopher Watts*. One thing I have learned is that those who have American Indian in their blood have a sort of sixth sense where they can, as one woman put it, "Read people's souls." I've always said, and my husband will attest, that I can spend fifteen seconds with someone and sum up who they are. That did not change when I saw Christopher standing on his front porch talking to the media, and I knew he was well aware of where his wife and children were and that he had murdered them. I also sensed a deep feeling of darkness from him, yet I didn't think darkness was always prevalent. I don't think Shanann saw it because he was smart enough to keep it hidden inside him. My belief is he knew it was there. I believe, by his admission to me, that he had horrible dark thoughts many times toward Shanann. He said there were times she was after him about something, and he wouldn't listen; he would look at her and think how he could kill her. These were dark thoughts long before he acted on them. Not for one moment did I ever think he was innocent. He did tell me they didn't fight. She would "go off" on him, he said, and he would not argue back or disagree with her. How much better for all had he been able to stand up to her?

However, through the last five years since he murdered his wife Shanann, daughters Bella and Cece, and son Nico, there have been millions of people weighing in on what happened. They were there as if they sat and talked to him and got the story as if they knew more than we knew. Like it or not, I was the one who did—the *only* one who did. He opened up to me and used me as his sounding board, and now, I'm also known as his *speaker*. He used me to get it all off his shoulders. Then, because of the fallout, he found it easier to blame me. He denied that he gave me the information to print in a book. I produced the signed agreement; if you want to see it, buy my book, *The Murders of Christopher Watts,* and you can see our signed notarized agreement and his letters. You will read in these letters what he wanted in the book. When the media and others caught sight of my book, it was a huge shock to some. Mostly, he killed his daughters "twice." These are his words. Christopher was never promised anything other than what was in my book. Shanann's parents were shocked, and that's something that surprised him. So, he found it easier to blame me. I have full proof of everything.

For those of you who are familiar with the Watts story, I will update and refresh the story. For those unfamiliar, read my book,

The Murders of Christopher Watts. Even though it has been five years since that fateful morning of August 13, 2018, the story is still as interesting and addictive as it was from the beginning. Causing millions of people to be drawn in a way they just can't let go. Not because Christopher is so good-looking, not because he's the first man to have an affair or even the first to kill his family. I believe it's so popular because so many people believe wholeheartedly that his mistress had something to do with it. Many believe she physically participated in the murders. In the chapters below, you will see why I feel she did play a part. I did not always believe this, and not until I did more research can I come to the conclusion I have now.

I don't think there has ever been such an attack on another author as there has been on me. I was just a regular person. I had not harmed anyone. I felt a call to write a book and to get the story straight from the killer himself. That's what I did. I took the initiative to write to him, form a relationship with him, go to the prison, and spend many hours sitting and talking face-to-face with a cold-blooded killer.

I think the whole thing went crazy when a woman contacted the Watts family with the intent of making money off the case and convinced Christopher's mother that he could not have possibly killed his family. Of course, a mother does not want to believe that of her son, and she was willing to grab onto any other theory of what could have happened. After all, Christopher did not even tell his family what had happened. She went as far as creating a YouTube channel where she charged people money to listen to a nonsense made-up story of things that made no sense. After making much money and leading the Watts family down a dead-end road, she dropped the family and all her nonsense. Leaving many people wondering what they had just been caught up in. People are so thirsty to get the truth that they could be sidetracked into believing something so far-fetched.

And there were so many others, and so far-fetched that I'm not going to give them the attention by mentioning their scams. It's a shame that someone invents such scams to take money from people trying to get to the bottom of a tragedy. I have been accused of just wanting money, and that's the reason I wrote my book. Let me tell you, I have worked hard—very hard. Not only did I drive three and a half to four hours away from my home to pay for hotel stays, but I have spent countless hours investigating, reading, writing, and talking face to face and on the phone day after day with a murderer. Am I not allowed to put it in a book? To help people understand what has happened. Why can other authors write about cases? I can't? Why? Because I'm new at writing? Every author had to have their first book. People could not stand that he gave me the story. I had no love interest in Christopher. It's just an interest to get the real story. Yet that road has led me down different paths to the truth.

That was cruel. I did not realize until very far into writing my book that the Watts family had never been told the truth of what happened. In fact, at one point, Christopher told his mother that she needed to wait for my book to come out, and then she could learn the truth of what happened. During this time, I was in contact with his mother, and she knew I had the truth. She told me she didn't know if she could handle the truth and wanted to wait until the book came out, only to blame me later. Yet, when this other woman came along with a different story, his mother was happy to grab onto her theory. However, at the time, this other person had never met Christopher and had never sat down to discuss the crime with him. She had found a way to turn the crime into money for herself, and she went to extremes to do that. Not caring who she stepped on or what means she had to go through to do it. She called *People's* Magazine, *Lifetime*, and many other places.

At every turn, I was told this woman had contacted them and tried to sell her narrative. These places she contacted looked at her as a "crazy person." That narrative soon became the "narrative of the Watts." When I would not pick up their narrative and write that in my book, I became the enemy. There was no stopping them; they went down every avenue they could to destroy me. I did not fight back; I did not stoop to the level of tearing others apart and lying and trying to destroy them or others. I had the facts straight from Christopher himself. At least, I thought I did.

What his family and many others would not acknowledge is the information I had fit the evidence the FBI had. There was not anything else that fit. Do we really believe the FBI and law enforcement would lie, cheat, and conjure up a completely false story? That just did not happen, nor would it make any sense. I absolutely detest the way Shanann is bashed. Who ever heard of bashing a victim of a murder? Especially a pregnant mother of two small girls who were also murdered. It seems to some that she deserved it in some way. There is nothing she could have done to Christopher or his mother to deserve what she was dealt. When you put your mind to it, you can feel the intense sadness of what happened to her and her children—the finality of all of it. Personally, I can cry when I give it much thought. Then, she attacks her family the way some have done. It's amazing and inexcusable. After losing my grandson, I can only imagine their pain.

Christopher and Shanann's house sat empty for almost five years. The eeriness of the house seemed haunted by the spirits of Shanann and her children. A home that once was full of laughter, happiness, and, yes, love was now an empty shell. No longer a home, just a house. Many YouTube creators filmed outside of the home, claiming to see the girls come to the window. As we all looked, our imagination could see them standing there. It's because our minds could picture the sweet little girls looking out their bedroom windows or Shanann walking past a window as she performed her daily chores. They were casting a scary and chilling scene over this once beloved home. Every movement that went on inside and outside of the house was captured by someone who put it on YouTube. Now, the house is a home again as it is occupied by a loving family. There can't be any ghosts there; Shanann and her babies were not evil, but now the evil spirit, soul, and body dwell in the Wisconsin Prison.

Christopher told me the night after the murders when he spent the night alone there, many things happened. "I sensed an evil spirit that plagued me," he said—"waking up to all the lights being turned on in the middle of the night." He said this is why he stayed with friends the next night. He feared being alone in the house where he had wreaked so much horror. This brings me to why he felt so much evil.

Christopher betrayed everyone in his life. His wife, children, parents, sister, in-laws, and all their friends. Friends that had welcomed him into their home right after the murders because they believed in his innocence. What could possibly make a man do that? Interestingly, again, even some of Shanann's friends have been attacked. How is it that the hero of the story was brutally attacked during a time of grief and health problems? What has become of us to be able to behave in this manner? Why was this crime, these murders, any more important than all of the other crimes and murders that happen on a daily basis? Why Christopher? He is certainly no one of any more importance. The true hero is Nichole Atkinson, and the beloved are Shanann, Nico, Bella, and Cece. The villains are, of course, Christopher and NK.

So why did so many of us become so enthralled in this particular story? People, mostly women, have become almost obsessive with it. So many have written to him; they feel like they love him. There has been at least one relationship with him that destroyed a marriage and family. I have had countless people contact me, asking how they can get in touch with him. *He's a murderer*, people! There is no worse murderer than annihilating your family, children, and pregnant wife.

I am not the only one who was being destroyed by these people. It didn't matter who you were. If you did not align with their theory, they attacked you, whether it was other authors or someone with their YouTube channel. What is interesting is many of the people who were being attacked were led by his family.

One of the best YouTube creators, in my opinion, is Armchair Detective. He worked countless hours to put the story together. He was able to find evidence the police didn't have or care about because they already had enough evidence to find him guilty, and Christopher made a plea of guilt on all charges. He entered that plea so he didn't have to stand a lengthy trial where he would have to see pictures and hear all he had done. He also pleaded guilty because he did not want to be sentenced to death. He cannot stand to hear out loud what he did. What is interesting to me is how the very murderer is so afraid of death. I hope he can come to a place of serenity in God and that he looks forward to going to Heaven instead of fearing hell. Because I believe in God, forgiveness, and Heaven, and as heinous as his crime is, we all have sinned, we are all offered forgiveness, and none of us deserve it.

My son once told me, and I agree: "It was man's law that saved Christopher Watts by sentencing him to life in prison." God's law would have been death for what he did. What I mean by that is God's law is that Christopher should have been executed for killing his family. Some would call it an "eye for an eye." Man saved him by giving him life in prison. My own opinion is he should have been executed, not that my opinion counts when I think of what those two little girls went through. Bella watched her sister being murdered by their daddy, whom they loved and trusted above all. The horror of Bella knowing she was next. Not knowing what it was that she had done wrong. Watching her daddy bury their mommy in a shallow grave. They wanted their mommy to wake up and save them from this horrible nightmare. The thoughts create a terrible monster in Christopher. His crime is not to go unpunished, but again, in my opinion, he should have given up his life to take theirs. Most people who commit such a heinous crime will commit suicide after killing their family. He told me he never considered that. Christopher is a narcissist; he would not kill himself. Although to the FBI, he made it seem he had given it thought. I assure you, he did not.

One of the puzzling things for everyone was why? Why did he do this? He had it all.

Sure, there were some problems, but not huge problems. No problem that couldn't have been solved by going to marriage counseling. Even if the problem seemed too big or he just couldn't live without his girlfriend, he should have left his wife and divorced her. I agree he knew Shanann was not the type of person who would let go easily. Why should she? After all, she was trying to protect her home, her children, their family, and her marriage. She had every right to do so. The girlfriend had no right to walk in and destroy and break up a family. That's for a different page. We will get there.

This idea was not authored by Christopher. He did not have the capacity to think of all of this by himself. I can tell you after spending the time I did with him and hours of talking on the telephone, this man did not come up with this idea by himself. We will probably never know who was the mastermind behind these ideas, but trust me, he was not the sole owner of them nor the originator of them. Again, later in this book, I do offer my opinion as to how this came to be, which leaves more questions as to who. Who put these ideas into his head? Was it a combination of people? Although I know he thought of killing them for some time. What triggered that? I feel I know, or at least I think. I'll let you, the readers, decide if my opinion fits the crime. He did not snap and, all of a sudden, kill Shanann. By his admission in his letters to me, he thought about it for a while. You can read his letters in *The Murders of Christopher Watts*.

I have tried to think in my own heart and head what drove him to this point. I cannot relate to why he did this, but I believe he was tired of the marriage he was living in and now feels he is in a better place than in his marriage. Not that he wants to be in prison, I don't mean that, but the fact he doesn't feel pushed around like he felt with Shanann. Had he just become a man and stuck up for himself, I truly believe she would have changed. I think Shanann wanted a take-charge husband, not one who was mean to her or bullied her around, but one who would step up to the plate and be a man. Christopher was not that person. So, in his head, instead of fighting with Shanann, it was somehow easier to get rid of her. Yet the children; why get rid of the children? The truth is he did not want to have the responsibility or the hassle of having a family. He told me once the thought of him being caught never entered his mind.

Here I go. I take the chance again to put my opinions and knowledge of the crime to the public view. I do hope you will accept it for what it is. Again, I'm trying to get to the truth. So, this book is about the different theories and stories out there. You may be shocked by this book, so hang on! Everything I state in this book is either my belief or my opinion of what Christopher told me. The research I did renders just my opinion, not facts.

So come along with me on this journey as I recap the murders, and follow Christopher on this ride; a ride he should have been sharing with NK in my belief.

CHAPTER 1

Refresh From The beginning

"Each of us is a book waiting to be written, and that book, if written, results in a person explained."

By: Thomas M. Cirignano

Let's start from the beginning. Christopher was an odd, quiet child who never (according to his mom) gave them any sort of trouble. He had a couple of close friends growing up, but he was not very sociable overall. He stayed to himself most of the time. His mother worked full-time, and he stayed with his maternal grandmother while his mother worked.

His grandmother was of German descent, without much emotion—hard and strict. She loved Christopher, and there was sometimes contention between her and Christopher's mother over how to raise him. Christopher loved her, though, and loved spending time with her. She may be the one that he inherited or learned his emotionless character from. The grandmother lived down the street from the Watts, so it was easy access for Christopher to go to her house. I was told it was not ideal that he spent so much time with her, but there was no real alternative. His mother worked, and dropping him by her mother's house was convenient.

As a teenager, he did not date. Many weekends, when his friends would be at school dances or out with their friends, Christopher would be at home with Mom and Dad, watching movies or doing whatever his parents would do; this was odd to his parents, but they passed it off as he was just a good boy. Christopher and his sister grew up in a South Carolina home. There were about eight years between them, but they were still close. His sister watched out for him. His sister and his mother babied him. A mama's boy who did what he was told. He didn't argue back or question what he was told—"the perfect teenager."

There was a time when he was a young teenager when his mom said she could hear him in the bathroom saying, "I'm sorry, I'm sorry, please forgive me!" She would ask him what he was talking about, but he wouldn't tell her. She once commented that she could always know what he was thinking. She would frequently ask him what he was thinking and what was on his mind. He would usually tell her, but not when he was in the bathroom asking forgiveness for something she did not know about. What could that have been? I think many of us could conjure up what it may have been. However, I'm sure we will never know. Is this just one of the things growing inside of this monster? These things may have simmered in his mind for years until it all boiled over that fateful night of August 13, 2018. The evil within him was bound to come out at some point.

The evil within him, I don't think, was ever seen by Shanann. She was completely blindsided by the evil thoughts and his ability to annihilate his family. During the murder, when his sweet little girl looked him in the eyes as he was killing her, it was, I'm sure, the first time she saw that evil monster face to face. During some of the years when he was growing up, his father was addicted to drugs. The family had to carry on and manage without him. Even though he was always in the house, he spent a lot of money on cocaine and other drugs. They lived a very modest life and seem to still. Christopher loved him all the same but had to carry on life without any real relationship with his dad during that time. His mother would attend church with the kids without their father. During that time, I'm assuming, is when he grew a conscience that would cause him to beg forgiveness for something he had been doing. I'm pretty sure it wasn't as simple as stealing a Matchbox car from the local Five and Dime.

One day as a young boy, Christopher was playing outside. He was with a couple of boys, and something happened that Christopher does not like to talk about. I'm not sure if it was another child or if it had to do with an animal; whatever it was, it was too shameful for him to talk about. Was this also what caused him to run to the bathroom and beg God for forgiveness? I don't know, and I'm sure the family isn't going to tell us either.

After Christopher graduated high school, he went on to NASCAR school. He graduated and saved his money. He was good with money and had good savings when he married Shanann. He dated very little until his cousin introduced him through Facebook to Shanann. He said he never thought she would give him the time of day. Yet his boyish charm and his kind personality won her over. He cared for her like no other man had before. Shanann had been married before to an attorney Leonard King, so she was a little more experienced in relationships than Christopher was. During that time, Christopher was a little overweight and, honestly, in my opinion, not very good-looking. He pursued Shanann; it was not the other way around. Whatever the things were that he said to Shanann, or maybe it was the things he did for her or the way he treated her, won her affection. At a family get-together at the beach, Christopher asked Shanann to marry him; she said yes. He gave her a beautiful diamond ring. His mother told me the ring was way too expensive, and he took the money from his savings to buy it for Shanann. His mother was furious that he would do that for this girl she was certain would break his heart. She had already broken his mother's heart.

After a couple of years of engagement, Shanann and Christopher were married. He told me the most hurtful thing his family ever did to him was not attending their wedding. Let's think about this. Here is a man who had been his mother's everything. He and Shanann planned a large, beautiful wedding, and at the last minute, because of a small disagreement between Shanann and his sister, they all made the mistake of not attending their wedding. This would have been so hurtful and so disappointing. Your child's wedding is so important that they can at least put their differences aside for one day and go to the wedding. This started hard feelings from the get-go. I'm sure at this point, Shanann just wanted to get away from his family.

From the first time the Watts family met Shanann, they did not like her. They predicted from the beginning the relationship would not work. In my opinion, they were not willing to give her a chance. They did not see at the time that she made him happy, and he made her happy. They were in love, and they desperately needed the support of their families.

Christopher especially needed his family's support. My opinion is if he had been offered their support and they had been kinder to Shanann; things could have been much different. I'm not saying the murders were their fault, at least not directly, but I think it's a possibility the murders may have never happened if there had been a better family dynamic. Christopher needed the confidence he could have gained from his family to have left Shanann instead of taking her life.

Sometimes, we are never ready for the cards we are dealt. We don't do things on purpose to have an outcome like a son killing his family. I doubt the Watts ever gave it an inkling of a thought that he was capable of doing such an awful act, something that would change all of their lives forever. Christopher may be physically in prison, but what he did to his family and Shanann's family is to put them all in a different kind of prison that they were also sentenced to for the rest of their lives. I find it very odd that Christopher told me one time, that he was not sure Shanann was in Heaven, because he didn't think she knew God. All I can say to that is, "Wow."

CHAPTER 2

"Unless Today is well lived, tomorrow is not important."

By: Alan Sakowitz

One of the theories about Christopher killing his family is that "the Watts" put the thoughts into his head or that they had a part in the murders. As I said, in my opinion, they had absolutely nothing to do with the very thought or actions of the murders. I say this with honesty, even though the Watts family has been brutal to me. His mother tried to destroy me in several different ways. However, I have empathy for what they have gone through. I believe if there is anything they did that could have been a part of what Christopher did, it was maybe his relationship with his mother. She encouraged him to write the letter and, if anything happened to him, to look at Shanann. Again, something he did not come up with on his own, but he was telling his mother and sister how unhinged Shanann was and he was uncertain as to what she might do. I believe laying the groundwork for what was to come.

My opinion is he always tried to please his mother. This came out when he would talk to me about what he had done, and he could not tell his mother—months turned to over a year before she knew the whole story. Because he wanted her to get the story by reading my book, he could blame me instead of owning up to his mother for what he had done. She took that lead and took it out on me, also. It's very odd, and I think it has to be left to a professional psychologist to explain. Their blame was also how they treated and felt about Shanann. Never could they have predicted that he would do something like this. I will talk later about this, but I think there was a direct influence, but not from his family. I think Christopher decided after there had been trouble between Shanann and his mother that he had to take the side of his mother. His mother commented once that Shanann took Christopher from them. Think for one moment what that means about a full-grown man.

Love can do many things. It can make us strong or weak, happy or miserable, smart or stupid, content or restless, angry or sad. It pulls at one's soul strings and sometimes can cause us to make decisions we would not normally make. Sometimes, we think it's love when it's infatuation or lust. Of course, we all know there are different kinds of love. The love for our spouse is very different than the love we have for our children. Real love is also very different from the love we have for a casual affair. Some love lasts a lifetime, some for a very short time. Another story I was told was when Christopher was eight years old, his sister accidentally shut the van door on his head. At one time, his mother told me she wondered if that accident could have caused some brain damage. Although I thought nothing was wrong with Christopher.

Christopher and his dad had one thing in common. They both loved race cars; it was the bond that kept them together in the years Christopher was growing up. They would travel to different cities to watch NASCAR races; this gave Christopher the idea that he wanted to go to NASCAR school and become a car racer himself; at the least, he wanted to become a mechanic for them. Thus, he enrolled and went to NASCAR school. I believe it was hard for the Watts to have a "normal" family life. Ronnie Watts was on drugs for several years. When the children were younger, their mother took them to church for a while. However, Ronnie did not go with them. When Christopher's sister was, I believe, seventeen, she left home.

Christopher played many sports: Baseball, football, and soccer. I think his father even coached some of his teams. However, according to Christopher, he didn't like sports. He was forced to play in them and also did it to please his father. I'm sure, by most people's accounts,

Christopher was a normal child; he looked normal and functioned normally, but I believe he was very abnormal.

During his teenage years, Christopher did not date. He stayed home with his parents on weekends and did not have a social life. For the most part, he had two close friends and, beyond that, did not seem to seek out any other friends. In my opinion, during his adolescent years, at the very least, Cindy should have taken Christopher to be tested for Autism. I do believe he could be on the lower spectrum of that. He even told me he wished he had been tested. I don't believe they will do those tests now that he is in prison. At this point, I don't think it matters. Yet it may have mattered a few years ago when he had a family. In talking with Christopher, he had no real social skills. He can't look you in the face when talking and is awkward at best. He realized he had social difficulty, and his mother told me he had asked her why he couldn't look people in the face when talking. If my son voiced that he was having social issues, I would have taken him to the doctor and asked for tests. In hindsight, I know there wasn't anyone in his circle of family and friends who would have known what he would grow up to be. Christopher was a people pleaser. He wanted to do what he was told to do, and he is still like that today in prison.

CHAPTER 3

When They Were Wed

"He loses his power when we know his face."

By: Michele Mcnamara

Sometime after his NASCAR graduation, Christopher met Shanann through his cousin. She was beautiful, fun, motivated, and very accomplished, everything a man would want in a wife. She already had a large, beautiful home of her own. All this information is in my book, *The Murders of Christopher Watts,* so I will not spend time on it here. There is a lot of controversy around Shanann having that house on her own. However, remember she was at one time married to an attorney. It's possible the money she got from her divorce built the home she was living in. We don't know, and it's none of our business, nor at this point it makes any difference.

They were married on November 3, 2012. On vacation one year, they went to Colorado to visit one of Shanann's friends. They loved it so much that they wanted to move there. It's easy to see why—Colorado is a beautiful state. With clean air and beautiful scenery, it's hard to go and not want to live there. They returned to South Carolina, put Shanann's house up for sale, and moved to Colorado. It was a huge shock for their family. His mother was very upset. She already didn't like Shanann, but now she had a reason to hate her. They moved in with one of Shanann's friends while they were having their house built. They were building a house fit for a king, way above their means. He said this house was something that Shanann had to have. He wasn't given a choice. He said the only thing about the house he picked out was the color of the siding and the brick on the front. Interestingly, the only two parts of the house I thought were unappealing.

While their house was being built, they moved in with Shanann's friend. He told me things did not go well. After a while, their differences became too much to get past. Whatever the problems were, they were large enough to end the friendship. Christopher wished they had never moved in with her friend because he would have liked to save their friendship. He said the problems were between Shanann and her friend.

When they bought the house in Colorado, it had to be put in Christopher's name.

Whatever the reason at the time, it could not have Shanann's name on it. I assume her name was added later. The house was a large, beautiful home with five bedrooms, a living room, two family rooms, a dining room, a kitchen, and breakfast seating—any young couple's dream home. Shanann had it decorated with modern décor. Beautiful and comfortable, a true home. Or at least they thought at the time. For a while, I believe love did reside there. They had Bella first, then along came Celeste (CeCe). It seemed like the *perfect* family that had everything.

Christopher had a good job at the Anadarko oil fields. He was a supervisor who got along with everyone, although he didn't interact much with people. His nickname at work was Silver Fox. When I saw Christopher in prison, he was almost all gray and kept his hair short.

I have talked with some of Shanann's friends. It was no secret that Shanann ran the show. Christopher said he always felt like he was in the background. When Shanann threw her dinner parties, she would tell him to take all the children upstairs and watch them. I think this is why no one really knew him. According to him, he wasn't allowed to socialize with everyone. However, he says he didn't care. He said life with Shanann was easiest if he did what he was told. He didn't disagree or push back. Yet, in his mind, he had murderous thoughts of a monster that would end up boiling over and spilling out.

Shanann was working from home for a company called Thrive. She made about $70,000 annually, and her sales were high enough to have a company-issued Lexus. However, she worked many hours per week and always devoted time to making that kind of income. From what Christopher told me, I sensed she was becoming weary of it. He hated her being on Facebook all the time and resented her putting him on live spontaneously. He said he went along with it to please and help her for her job.

In 2015, they had to file bankruptcy, and according to Christopher, they were headed there again. If it's correct, he said their bankruptcy was around 600K. He said he "felt bad because all Shanann could think about was money." They were in trouble, and it consumed her to keep everything afloat. Christopher said they were headed for bankruptcy again, but it was too soon to file again. She was juggling everything. Finances were out of control. He said he would bring home his paycheck, which would immediately disappear. They had started thinking about selling their home and downsizing. Something I believe Shanann did not want to do but was willing to do. They were being taken to court for their severely delinquent association fees; I think it was the month he killed her that they were to appear in court for the lawsuit.

The finances consumed her, but she didn't know how it affected him. He was angry inside that they were living like this when he said they didn't have to. Sex was on her terms, he said. So here is a marriage where the man feels unimportant and unheard, finances are totally out of control, and his physical and sexual needs are not being met—a recipe for failure. But failure for a man like Christopher was something much deeper, much more awful, and he, in his mind, had to do something to escape this life he was living.

I think toward the end, Shanann realized her marriage was in trouble. At that point, she was willing to sell the house and do whatever it took to make her husband happy. After all, it was never a problem with him before; he just went along with whatever. Why was he different now? Why had he changed? It was because he had a girlfriend that made him feel like his opinion counted and somebody heard him. *She listened to him; she understood him*—a *cliché.*

Another thing his mother told me is that Shanann was not allowed to be alone with her children. The Department of Family Services had to come to the home and determine if something was "going on"—this was nonsense! There was a fake document floating around. When I asked Christopher about this, he said it was untrue and didn't understand where this could have come from. And his mother had mentioned this to him, even telling him about this fake document. I know where this started; it came from the woman who befriended his mother, the one I wrote about earlier. Shanann did not have the Department of Family Services called on her. That was a fake document and a fabricated story.

This woman, whom I have spoken of earlier, was doing everything to try and prove her narrative. She wanted people to believe she had proof. Yet, if you listened to her "proof," she talked in complete circles, making no sense. Fabrication, bashing Shanann, blaming Shanann. Why? For money, not because she believed it. She was a total scammer. She caused many problems and hurt many people, then finally disappeared. If you've followed this case from the beginning, you know who I am talking about. However, she was the one person who started so many rumors and horrible things that were being spread on social media. This case did not lack its fair share of scammers. People with a thirst and hunger for revenge wanted to befriend the Watts, and when they listened to his family, they set out to prove Christopher did not kill his family. Again, it was all for clicks and views, which turned into what they hoped would be money. Some use this as their sole income, creating a dog-eat-dog platform. Never have I witnessed such lies and abuse as there was in the YouTube community. Their agenda is to ruin each other; the harder they can make it on a person, the more they love it, which scares me about this level of humanity. Where are we headed with such hate for each other?

So, why did Christopher take that route with his family? Now, if you talk to him, he wishes he was still with Shanann and his children. How could something be so powerful as to cause him to kill all of them? It's because he met NK. He also will tell you now that he can't believe he did something like this. Sitting in his cell one evening, where he could see the guard's television, he witnessed himself on the news. "What a huge blow," he said as he watched, not believing they were talking about him; he would never do such a horrible act.

Christopher told me he met NK at the gym where he worked out. When Shanann had neck surgery, her parents stayed with them to help them with the children. They were living in the downstairs unfinished basement. That's where Christopher usually worked out. He joined a health club since he couldn't work out while they were living with them. I believe it was there in 2017 that he met NK.

On the evening of July 4, 2017, Shanann, Christopher, and the girls went to the city fireworks. They were there as a family for an evening of fun and relaxation. He told me that NK came up, said hello, and introduced her to Shanann. I believe she could have been stalking him. I don't think that was a coincidence. My belief is she was fascinated with Shanann. We know she had searched for Shanann on social media sites. It became like a game; she wanted to see if she could take this man from his family. I believe he also would tell her where he was going with his family, and she would show up there—maybe seeing how close she could get to him. I do not believe it's as simple as Christopher just met Nickki at work, as many people have always thought. I do believe she chased him from the very beginning. I also believe she was unhinged and would have gone to any extent to have Christopher.

CHAPTER 4

The Gentle Murderer

"They shared a doom against which virtue was no defense."

By: Truman Capote

I believe NK was enamored by the way Christopher treated her. I think he was kind and gentle and was very used to the women in his life being the leader of the relationship. Not long before she was with Christopher, she had gotten out of a bad relationship. The relationship may have been abusive. Little did she know Christopher was capable of murder. I think he fell for her so quickly because of two things: one was the kind of sex she would provide him, and the other was that she knew exactly how to play him. She would allow him to make decisions and encourage him to lead their relationship, but little did he know this was the worst kind of control.

There was a very small window when Christopher felt tired of NK. However, she was able to pull him toward her. He told me she was like a magnet. He could not resist her. Had he given everything more time, I think he may have murdered her instead of his family. He didn't know how to break off a relationship in the right way.

On July 4th, 2018, NK and Christopher were at her apartment. Shanann kept texting and trying to call Christopher. He said she was intent on talking to him, and he was worried she suspected something. NK was in the shower, so he told her he was going home for the afternoon. However, she could not allow him to be alone with his thoughts, and she showed up at his door. To me, this was a moment of decision for Christopher. He even thought about it here; he said he "was feeling tired of the relationship." She came into his house; he said, "She looked around and went upstairs and looked at pictures" while he was fixing them some lunch. She came downstairs and asked him why he would give all of this up. She seemed upset, and I think she was feeling insecure and jealous. As she looked around this beautiful house, she could see all he and Shanann had built, plus the two little girls they had.

Supposedly, she did not know about Shanann's pregnancy. I believe that this is not true because, during that visit, he and NK got into an argument. He said she went out to her truck and was texting him. After a few texts, he said he became annoyed and told her to "come back into the house." As they were talking, and in his words, he "talked her off the ledge," she told him she "wanted to give him his first son." They had sex on the kitchen counter, because he said "she wanted to leave her mark." She became upset, telling Christopher she wanted him to decide; this tells me a lot about whether or not she knew about Shanann's pregnancy. In my opinion, she knew, and she wanted him to do something. Is this possibly laying plans in his head? Remember, he tried to cause her to miscarry, after much research and talking to not only Christopher but his family; my belief is he got the Oxy from NK. Christopher, remember, is not your "average" kind of guy. So, my belief is this started his wheels churning.

In my opinion, NK getting a job with Anadarko was planned. I believe she applied there because she knew Christopher worked there. It was easy then to start pursuing him. Once she started to have a relationship with him, she would stalk Shanann on social media. That was easy because she was on Social Media a lot, after all, that was her job. He said they flirted and played around for a while. He asked her to go to a park with him one day after work. I believe they had sex on this day, as he did say they started having sex almost immediately after going out. They started to get closer. It surprised him that NK seemed to be coming after him. He said women did not usually pursue him, so when NK did, it was a turn-on for him. He said he had a decision to make. During this time, he went on a trip with Shanann that she had earned for her work. He said he did not want to go, and all he could think of was NK while he was gone. There is a video that Shanann had made of them in their hotel room; you could tell he was not happy about being there or being filmed— this was the beginning of the end. Christopher started planning Shanann's demise. He said he started thinking of different ways to kill her. I have to wonder if he had those feelings toward NK, too. I think he was having these thoughts, but when NK started talking to him about getting out of the relationship, it started to move his thoughts and plans forward.

When we started talking about NK and those few weeks, it became clear that he had a sexual addiction; this was not an addiction he could satisfy with Shanann. Shanann was a mom and a wife, not a sleazy sex object. I believe that Shanann called the shots. She told him what to do, but he was also very used to that and just complied. He got tired of it and daydreamed about what it would be like if he killed her and got rid of her; this was well before he met NK. What did NK do to give him the courage to carry out his dream? Was it the sex he had with her? By his account, their sex was beyond what he wanted. She made him feel like a man; she met the desires of the sexual perversion that he had. However, it never would have lasted. I will lay out my idea and theory of why and how NK had so much control over him.

Right before Shanann went to spend time with her family in North Carolina, she found out and told Christopher she was pregnant. The day he decided to go ahead with the affair with NK was when Shanann told him about her pregnancy. In the video posted online, you can see the shock and disdain on his face. There was no way for him to hide it. I'm sure Shanann must have known, and what a disappointment she must have felt.

While Shanann innocently visited her parents and in-laws, Christopher was lying and deceiving her daily. It was hard for Shanann at times to get in touch with Christopher. He was working by day and playing by night. Weekends were fulfilling their desires as they camped, went to car races, and did all the things a single couple would do. There is one text string between NK and Christopher where she wanted to visit the mountains together for a few days. He told me he hardly thought of his family; this is not normal during this time, as most men would be consumed with guilt.

When I think of the level of lying and deception Christopher did, it makes me feel physically ill. Shanann loved him, and I believe she was true to him. Christopher's mother started very ugly rumors about Shanann and another man, which, in my opinion, were made up. I know this for certain because she told me those things. Many people may do harmless flirting at conferences or other work events, but it doesn't go any further than that. I don't understand people who hate someone enough to make up lies and cause that person's reputation to be scared. I know about that; I've had plenty of that myself. People have been obsessed with making up lies about me, but imagine how awful it is that a woman is murdered, and people spread ugly lies and accusations about her. To the point that even her family is being put through hell. The level of evil has no match for this type of thing.

Shanann left at the end of June to visit her family in North Carolina. He was free! He felt like a bachelor. He was free to be with NK without sneaking around or lying about where he was. It was a dream for him to have as much time with her as he wanted. He and NK went on a camping trip in the mountains. They had dinners and went to the car races. They spent a lot of time in bed together. During the time that Christopher was playing house with his mistress, he brought her into his and Shanann's home. I believe they were in bed together there. According to him, they had sex several times a day. I also believe he had her over to his house several times, not twice like he says in his letters to me.

Some of their sexual acts were so perverted that he told me there were things he would never talk about. Some things he will "take to his grave." One of those things has to do with the sexual things that went on. There were threesomes; they played with objects, they had anal sex. If he was looking for a way to feed the sexual desires he had, this was the person to do it with. They had threesomes, and I believe orgies. I've always believed from the things he said, that Jim was involved in those, now I also believe her friend Charlotte was also one of the players in that. I also believe that during this time he had a gay sexual encounter. I'm not sure with whom, but I feel pretty sure it was one of NK's friends.

Now, I know there are NK supporters out there, but these are the things Christopher told me. I have to also wonder how a man with this type of sexual desire can function in prison. I also wonder if these kinds of men are not getting their desires met; is that part of what builds the monster inside of them? After spending five weeks with his mistress, Christopher flew to North Carolina to spend time with his family. He did not want to go and said at first, he thought NK would make things easier for him by understanding what he had to do. But on his way to the airport, she texted him that she didn't want him to go; this was a mixed message that confused him.

There was a picture taken and sent to me by his mother. That picture was of a clear storage bucket in Christopher's basement. You could see bandages, gauze, and a medicine bottle like you would see from any pharmacy. His mother told me that it was Oxy that had been in the basement, and Shanann took it—implying that Shanann was addicted to Oxycodone.

Christopher and I talked about the Oxycodone he gave Shanann while in North Carolina. He said he gave it to her to make her miscarry. Obviously, it was a big deal to him because the first time I saw him in prison, one of the first things he asked me was if there was a big rumor about it. I told him it was a big deal and asked where he got it. He told me that was one of the things he would take to his grave. He was very clear about the oxy not coming from his basement; another rumor started by his mother. He also told me that Shanann did not take Oxy. She had been given a prescription once after her neck surgery; this is not the same Oxy he gave her. Again, I think he got the Oxy from NK.

One evening, according to a media outlet, they had Christopher on the telephone saying he got the Oxy from the basement. I called the prison to ask them about that particular phone call recording. It did not happen. That was a hoax, I presume, by his family. I believe it was to try and take the accusations off of them. I don't believe it worked; I think it made things worse. In my opinion, his sister did not give him the Oxy. Interestingly, the week just before the murders, NK got a visit from her long-time friend Jim Gutoski. He did not stay at her house but spent a good deal of time with her during his stay. Many people have suspected that he had something to do with the murders. However, he is not mentioned in the discovery, and he was never interviewed. This brings a question to why her friend Charlotte Nelson was mentioned. They did question NK a few times about Charlotte. Charlotte is a long-time friend of NK who lives a lesbian lifestyle. Was she the person who participated in the three-some with NK and Christopher?

CHAPTER 5

The Stalker

"I'm so glad you woke me. I was having the worst nightmare. I felt like I was suffocating. I dreamed the Devil was trying to choke me to death."

By: Jeanne Walker

I cannot stress enough that, in my opinion, NK stalked the Watts family a lot. I believe she was obsessed with Shanann and breaking up his family. We know she broke up his family and influenced Christopher with her sexuality. Another thing I have come to realize is NK hopped on a plane and went to South Carolina. I don't think she stayed the entire week, maybe just the weekend. I believe when Christopher left his wife in the evenings and disappeared for hours, he was meeting with NK. I believe the night he gave her Oxy and then left the house, he also was with NK. I don't know what happened with law enforcement, but possibly they cut a deal with NK that if she would tell them all she knew, she would be given immunity. Again, this is my belief; I have no proof. However, we know that Law Enforcement allowed her to run the content of the interview. NK talked non-stop, and there was no real interrogation. In the next chapter, I have put her entire interview in here. You will see how they just sort of surface-talked with her, allowing her to control the interview, giving no real information. Also, Christopher does not know the answer but believes it could be what happened. When I first met Christopher, he was still very much in love with NK.

We must remember that when I met with Christopher, he had no idea what was being said. He had no way of reading or watching television. He was in protective confinement and was completely unaware of everything except what his family told him on his fifteen-minute calls. There were many times he did not even get those calls. I had forgotten this when I met with him, and it amazed me at first how much he didn't know. In many instances of what was in the media, I had to tell him what was being said. Some of those things, I believe, cloud his memory because he didn't remember many things that were being said in the news.

In the beginning, he acted confused over some things they were reporting, saying he had no memory of them. Many of the theories were alarming to him. However, I realized later this is part of why I'm saying "The Many Faces of Christopher Watts." I used to think he was lying to me about remembering, but when you read on, you will see I think there was a very real reason that he might not have remembered everything.

When I went to the Dr. Oz show, I met Melissa Moore. Her father was the Happy Face Killer. She and I have remained friends. She told me that everything she had been through, it's typical for these murderers to think they are so much smarter than everyone else and play mind games with us. I learned that's exactly what Christopher was doing to me, and since then, I have seen how he plays mind games with many women who write to him. Some believe him so much that they will defend him to me. It's interesting how women who write to him will message me to let me know and see what I think about their correspondence with him. They all believe he has changed and are telling them the truth now until they realize he isn't. He knows how to play them and even causes them to feel sorry for him. He is a player at the very best.

Christopher told me that when they were at the beach in North Carolina, the girls would hardly have anything to do with him. He told me he felt it was because their pure spirits could sense the evilness that existed in him. To me, this goes back to the evilness he says he acquired while spending time with his mistress. If it's true that

NK made a drink for him called "Devil's Breath," then it's possible the evil effects still were in him at the time of the murders; this is something he truly believes. Some will say it is just him casting the blame on someone or something else, but is it?

Many things seemed to happen in North Carolina that added to the feelings Christopher was having toward Shanann. Of course, we know about "nut-gate" and the part his family played in that. It was awful how they treated Shanann because she protected CeCe from her allergy. Christopher said she did have an allergy to nuts. I questioned him about what happened when she ate nuts. He said she broke out in a rash and had difficulty breathing.

Honestly, I was appalled that his mother told me that CeCe, having an allergy was made up. His family did not support Shanann or their staying together. With two little girls and another child on the way, why was his family so against Shanann? Most parents would want their son to stay with his family and make things work. We've seen so much evidence to the contrary, and I can tell you, having spoken with his mother many times, she absolutely hated Shanann.

If we have ever been with a person who is very aloof toward us, then we know how uncomfortable it is. Christopher told me he looked back and realized how he made Shanann feel when treating her so cold that entire week they were together in North Carolina. When I think about that, it makes me sad. I momentarily put myself in Shanann's shoes and remembered how important my relationship was with my husband when I was pregnant. A woman needs to feel close to her husband and may even need extra attention when her body changes, and we aren't so secure about ourselves. During that time, we need reassurance from our husband to tell us we are beautiful and that being pregnant turns him on. Shanann just didn't understand what had changed him so much. She asked him over and over if there was someone else, and he continually told her no. She had never known him to lie to her before, so I believe she was confused. A woman never feels closer to her husband than when she is pregnant; now, the man she loved so much was treating her cold and indifferent. As I have said, here is an almost five-month pregnant woman who died hearing that her husband doesn't love her. How cruel her last few moments of life were so torturous.

During Shanann's visit with her in-laws, there was a really big argument. He told me that his mother disregarded Shanann's wishes and also disregarded the fact that Cece did have a lot of allergies. I asked him what would happen to Cece when she ate nuts or other things Shanann said she was allergic to. He said she would break out in hives and have difficulty breathing. When he told me this, it seemed to make him angry that his mother did not respect Shanann's advice about their daughter. My opinion was this happened a lot over different things, and Shanann had just had enough of it and couldn't contain herself any longer. I believe she was the kind of woman used to having her way, but after all, this was her children. There are times, as grandparents, we may not always agree with how our children do things, but it is their life, after all, and their children.

When the week was over, Christopher, Shanann, and the girls flew back to Colorado. Was NK on that flight with them? That following Friday, Shanann had plans to go to a Thrive convention. She was so concerned about her marriage that she told Christopher she would cancel her plans. He told her not to cancel her plans and that they could talk when she got home. She kept her plans but made travel arrangements for them to go to Aspen, Colorado, for the following weekend. Shanann was going to spend that time working on her marriage. Poor girl never got that chance. She never knew who her competition was, the woman who wrecked their family and led to the death of her and her three babies.

I can't imagine the gut pain and feeling Shanann must have had the day she left for the weekend in Arizona. It was a time that was supposed to be fun and a time of awards for the hard work she had put into her job. She deserved that weekend but didn't deserve what she walked into that Sunday night, early Monday morning of August 13, 2018.

CHAPTER 6

Bad Theories

"Behavior is the mirror in which everyone shows their true image."

By: Criminal Minds

Now is where we get to the truth and theories. Everything Christopher Watts confessed to me is in my book, *The Murders of Christopher Watts*. If you have not read it, I suggest doing so. There, you can read a copy of his letters where he confesses to me things he had not even told the FBI. Later, he would accuse me of not putting his testimony in the book; however, I did. He wrote about his testimony, and he was never deceived or manipulated. Again, he chose to blame someone else; this time, it happened to be me. He knew from the very first letter he received from me that I wanted to write a book about this story. Later, when we met, I made it clear I would be the last say about what went into the book. Retrospectively speaking, I was kind to him and his family. I never had any intention but to be kind to Shanann and her family.

I was contacted by someone using an alias that fed me a theory she claimed was coming from Christopher himself. This woman was on many panels on YouTube about the case and had a large voice. She told me that Christopher wanted it to be known that NK and her friend Jim did have a part in the murders. Here is what she said happened: "Nicole and Jim were at the house before Shanann got home. They were waiting for her and planned to help him kill all three of them. Supposedly, NK hid in the refrigerator in the basement, and Jim hid somewhere in the basement."

This theory says NK murdered Bella and Cece. Christopher supposedly told this woman that he did kill Shanann, but Jim was there to help carry Shanann out of the house. He supposedly parked out back on the other side of the fence. He said a new home was built, but no one lived there yet. After all three were murdered, they wrapped Shanann in a blanket and carried them downstairs when the girls woke up. This person told me that Jim helped Christopher carry Shanann's body out back and put her in NK's car. Supposedly, he grabbed the girls and put them in his truck. Once they arrived at the oil field, he dug a grave for Shanann, and NK killed Bella and Cece, and she and Jim put them in the oil batteries.

Once they arrived at the oil field, he proceeded to dig a grave for Shanann. Nk killed Bella and Cece, and she and Jim put the girls in the oil batteries. I believe this was just an attempt by this woman to implicate NK. As far as I know, no evidence supports this theory. Even though this woman says she knows Christopher well and he told her these things, I believe it was all conjured to give her some relevance. I do not believe Christopher told her these things; according to him, he does not even know her.

So why so many theories? People cannot get to the truth; there are some different scenarios, and some would make a good movie. However, none of them fit the evidence in this case. I do believe NK was by his house that morning. Maybe to see if Shanann came home or if she could tell that he talked to her about separating. Maybe it was because she was stalking them, and I believe she stalked the family.

The woman who gave me this theory always talked about how she and Christopher were good friends before the tragedy. She would talk about their phone calls and letters between them. I realized she was obsessed with him and the case. Why? Why so many people could not stop the craze?

I believe this woman is responsible for spreading so many theories and lies about this crime. Whether she got the idea from someone or if she just made it up, who knows, but it spread over social media like crazy. She would tell me she knew NK personally, and NK had decided to confess and turn herself in. One day, she told me NK would call and tell me the truth about what happened. I trusted her; she came at me like a friend and wanted to be trusted. I am not a hater, and I do trust easily. I was easy prey for her, and she took advantage of me with her lies. What makes people like this? I hope she is reading this because I want her to know how disgusting she is and that she plays with pure evil. She caused me to almost shut everything down. Had it not been for the lovely and kind people on my Facebook group, I would have.

I received some sound advice from people who are on television and entertainment. Those people helped me to prepare and beware of people like this woman. There is something about this case that makes it like none other. It brings out the ugly in people. This woman called me on the phone and told me NK was in the process of turning herself in. She messaged my Admin Brandi and tried to set her up. She harassed me so much that I should have turned her in to the police.

Another story that someone told me is about Cece being put in the refrigerator in the basement and Bella in a plastic tub after he had killed them. I don't believe this happened, but I know the dogs picked up a scent near that refrigerator. All while Christopher was waiting in the living room to attack Shanann as soon as she walked in the door. We know this is not true, as Shanann was on the computer ordering shampoo when she got home; this is a fact unless it was Christopher making it look like Shanann was on her computer. These are just all speculations. I feel there is no basis for most of them.

It could be true that Christopher doesn't remember everything had he been drugged, as you will read my theory in the following chapters. However, if he doesn't remember everything, how do you explain how he was able to write me the very detailed letters he wrote? Something, though, did have him horribly terrified enough that I do believe his account of seeing his grandparents in his jail cell. If you want to read about that story again, refer to my book, *The Murders of Christopher Watts.*

It is a horrifying story that I feel very sure is real to Christopher. Was he still having side effects from the drugs, or was it just the horrible trauma of the murders? I'm sure most of us cannot in a million years imagine killing our babies and putting them in oil batteries if you look at the whole story where Christopher was concerned: a good father, a good husband, a good friend. It doesn't add up that he could murder, especially his babies.

The horror that Cece and especially Bella experienced doesn't go along with the Christopher that everyone knew. That is why I believe something had to have happened to allow him to have done something like this. He gave up everything he had worked so hard for. Not a lot of men have accomplished as much at thirty-three years old. Could it be he was willing to give it all up for the likes of NK? It doesn't seem likely, does it? Yet he says had it not been for her, he would not have done everything he did; however, what did not only cost him the lives of his precious family, Shanann, Bella, Cece, and Nico. It cost him his own life. It forever injured and changed the lives of his in-laws, parents, and sister. It ruined some of their lives, but I can guarantee they will never be the same, and poor Rzuecks will live with unimaginable pain for the rest of their lives. All of this for NK is very hard to believe.

These murders have affected so many people. I have a Facebook group of just 3,500 people. I can tell you it has affected so many of their lives. We all ask ourselves how this could have happened. How is it that a normal husband could do this? And to most, the puzzle pieces do not fit. I have the most amazing Facebook group—a group of non-haters who have come together and researched this case to find the truth. Yet we are all still at the same stand-still we were five years ago.

CHAPTER 7

NK's New Name

"To get away with murder you simply don't tell anyone."

By: Criminal Minds

I have found out about NK's new name and where she lives. It has taken tremendous research, but I am 100 percent sure I know who she is. I was sent confirmation by someone who only wants to be referred to as Penny Lane. She did extensive research and was able to trace back NK through her voting records. It's odd that my research led us to the same place. However, when I saw how she traced her back, it was indisputable. My attorneys have advised me that publishing her name could open me up to some hard times. We all know how the media can be and how rough on people they can be. What if I'm wrong and some poor woman is hassled horribly? Or what if it is NK, and her father decides to come after me for releasing her name? After talking with my family, the decision has been made not to put her name in this book. Honestly, knowing her name isn't going to change anything for us, but it could turn her life into turmoil. I will tell you one interesting bit of information. Her new middle name is Lee. That is Christopher's middle name, so that says something. I'm sorry to disappoint so many of you, but this decision was made after the book was completed. It's been a very hard choice for me to make.

I think she gave Christopher "Devil's Breath." She wanted to confuse and control him. He has told me she was in the area the morning of the murders. I believe her vehicle was even parked outside for a while. I also feel the drink had something to do with giving him the courage to kill his family. To me, this is a conspiracy to commit murder. However, this drink takes the memory of a person, and he cannot accuse her because he does not definitely remember.

In my opinion, law enforcement should open this case back up and do more research on her and what she may have done. I do not believe they thoroughly investigated NK. In my opinion, they do not know about her past life. Once Christopher confessed and they located the bodies of Shanann, Bella, and Cece, I believe at that point, they were so sickened by what had happened they felt there was no further need to investigate. After all, Christopher insisted NK had nothing to do with the murders. It's possible he really believes this, as I feel he may have still been under the influence of some of those drinks. Don't get me wrong, he knew what he was doing was horribly wrong. He always said it was like he knew what he was going to do but couldn't stop himself. Was that a way for him to blame other things besides himself? The one thing that has always worked on me is if NK could have caused this. Again, I do not believe Law Enforcement looked any further since Christopher led him to the bodies. They felt they had their man, and they did.

Going back to June, Christopher made a conscious decision to start seeing NK. He said the day he decided to see her was the day Shanann told him she was pregnant with their third child. His family was not happy with the fact that Shanann was pregnant again. They wanted him out of that marriage and knew if she was pregnant again, it would prolong things. I believe that having NK as a girlfriend and his family against another pregnancy led to a lot of his thoughts turning to terminating her pregnancy and murdering his family. He felt justified, after all.

It was not long after Shanann left for her parents. I don't think she was feeling well, and the thought of having help with the girls during a time when she was feeling run down was appealing to her. However, that left Christopher to roam free, actually pretending to himself he didn't have any responsibilities. Now is when he could "play" with NK. I believe she took full advantage of Shanann being away and pulled Christopher toward her. He said he physically felt tugged toward her, like he had someone standing on each side of him, pulling him in opposite directions. In my opinion, NK did not have nearly as much going for her as Shanann did. However, Shanann was a mother and wife and was busy with everyday responsibilities. She didn't have time to feed Christopher's ego. She didn't realize she needed to; after all, they were married with children, and she thought they were on the same path.

NK searched for wedding dresses online. She was planning a life with Christopher, which was clear, yet she told the police she hardly knew him. People would talk about Christopher looking online for a diamond. He was not shopping for a diamond; he was looking for a specific crystal that NK wanted. He had hoped to surprise her with it.

During the time Shanann was away, Christopher and NK had sex several times a day. So as not to get bored with their sex, she tried to come up with different things to keep him turned on. Also, she was willing to do almost anything in the sex department.

We can only use our imaginations to come up with what he meant. I have a feeling it was so disgusting it could make anyone blush. It certainly was a subject Christopher became uneasy talking about. He seemed ashamed to even think back at some of the things that happened. My opinion is there were more than a three-some. I think it was more like couples, possibly more like an orgy. She had piqued the curiosity of a friend by telling her how good Christopher was in bed. I was told later by someone who did have knowledge that, in actuality, she was disappointed in his size, and it was hard to get the pleasure she really wanted. So, he would perform oral sex on her, which was very satisfying to her. I don't think it was about the sex for NK; I believe it was more about the game of breaking up Christopher's family that meant the most to her. For some people, this very thing turns them on, thinking that the mystery of being with someone else's husband is very appealing.

I was also told by Christopher that his girls met NK. Supposedly, they took them to the park one day, and he pretended like NK was just another person at the park. He said she talked to the girls and questioned them. Of course, he never acted to his girls like she was a friend. This way, they would not have anything to tell their mom, and if they did, Christopher could just pass it off as any person sitting at the park; this is another huge lie that was told to the authorities. Of course, she met Bella and Cece. I believe they probably were together with the girls several times. Another haunting thing that has come to light is some of the horrible things that went on the morning of the murders. Some do not believe this, but I promise you the girls were alive when he left the house.

Since he was not successful in killing them at home, he had to do that on-site; he said this was a very ugly scene. Bella fought him as hard as her little body could. I do not believe he killed her in the truck. My opinion is one or both of them were still alive when he got to the top of the stairs. From some of the things he told me, I thought one of them may have even been alive when he put them in the battery; however, the autopsy report does not show that. He ran out of time and knew his co-workers would be showing up for work soon; this is part of why I believe he had help at the oil site. He could not have had enough time to do all of that by himself. I don't believe NK killed either of the girls, but that is something the FBI needs to thoroughly investigate. However, if she was on the scene, then she was a part of it.

The autopsy—this brings me to another thought. I believe there are two autopsy reports, the one that can be released to the public and the one that was not released to the public. I think the true horror of the report is so gruesome they did not want the general public to see the entire report.

We know that their bodies were so oil-soaked they couldn't even have a regular funeral. Grandparents were not allowed to see them because of the condition of their bodies. They were considered flammable, so this tells us what a horrible state they were in. The amount of skin slippage and the condition of their bodies were enough to send even the most seasoned of law enforcement agents to counseling.

Nicole met Christopher at Anadarko; however, she was employed with Tasman Geosciences, and they contracted her to Anadarko in April 2018. By this time, she and Christopher had become friends through the gym they were both going to. My belief is he referred her to Anadarko. Possibly, her father had something to do with her finding employment with the Tasman Company.

Here is where things get a little murky. Was NK at Cervi the morning of the murders? I do know he had planned on blowing up the field. Who gave him the idea? He had a can of gas in the back of his truck. This is the kind of idea that does belong to the monster. We all saw him put that can in his truck through the neighbor's camera. I believe part of her mind control over Christopher was this sort of stuff. That's why, according to him, he was leaving Cervi that morning when he received a text from NK telling him to listen to the lyrics of the song by Metallica, "Battery." If you have not listened to that song, you will be shocked at how exact the song is to what happened. You would think if you didn't know better that NK wrote the song. I would be against copyright laws if I put the words in the book here, but please google it and read the words. It will give you chills.

NK did not go to work the morning of August 13. Why not? If she didn't know what was going on, why wouldn't she have just gone to work like any other day? It is my belief that her company fired her because they put things together and felt she played a part in the murders. They didn't want to be dragged through so much, and they certainly would not have tried to help her out. Christopher told me the ninety-minute phone call they had on Sunday evening was phone sex; later, he would say that was not their conversation. I am pretty sure there were some very heated words between them that night. I think she was demanding he get rid of Shanann. I do not believe she was telling him to kill Shanann. Because he has a simple mind and because he was always trying to please a woman in his life, he thought this was the best way. I think that is what he meant when he laid the girls down that night and said he knew that was the last time he would ever tuck the girls in. Either way, I think they discussed and argued about him doing something about his marriage. Was it more about how she could downplay their relationship so the police did not know there was a sorted affair going on? Or so it would protect her. After all, that is the reason she ran to the police as soon as she could, to make herself look innocent.

I think one of the reasons there has been so much bad social media concerning NK is the level of her deception, then running away and hiding; that's exactly what she did, a coward who is hiding in plain sight. If she had nothing to hide, it would be uncomfortable for her, but she would not have totally disappeared. She became one of the most hated woman in the world by running away. People may have been able to forgive her had she stayed and faced the music. After all, many women have affairs, and unfortunately, many break up homes. If she, in fact, had nothing to do with the planning, thinking, or executing of the murders, she should have stuck around. She googled Amber Fry, so she knows how Amber faced what was going on and apologized on her part for what Scott Peterson did. It only has made NK look more guilty that all she did was run from the public. Nothing to hide? Then why hide?

NK was at Christopher's house much more than he was willing to tell us in the beginning. If you watched the police cam when they were first in his house, you would see a bag at the bottom of the stairs. In that bag were NK's clothes. She knew every inch of that house, slept in Shanann's bed, and even used some of Shanann's products. What a travesty that Shanann was never able to know her competition. Had she, she would have won. Maybe that's what Christopher was afraid of. Shanann was ten times the woman NK is. This brings me to how anyone can bash a murdered woman and her murdered babies. I just can't phantom what kind of person it takes.

Some rumors on social media say that Christopher has gotten letters from NK since he has been in prison. I can assure you he has not received anything from her, and he has no idea her new name or where she is. I think she is hiding from him as much as she is from us. She does not want to face him, I assure you.

CHAPTER 8

Interview With NK And Law Enforcement

Following is a recorded interview the police had with Nichole Kessinger. I know that this is a long interview, but to get a real feel for NK, her personality, and how she handles this case, I suggest you read all of it. It's a fast read; in my opinion, you can see how it's all about her.

INTERVIEW WITH NICHOL KESSINGER
Interviewer: Agent Kevin Koback, Agent Tim Martinez
8-16-18
Case #2018-273

INTERVIEW WITH NICHOLE KESSINGER

Q=Agent Kevin Koback
Q1=Agent Tim Martinez
A=Nichol Kessinger
A1=Duane Kessinger

Q: Audio, um, we introduced ourselves in the lobby and - earlier so we're just gonna do that again real quick. My name's Kevin Koback, I'm with the Colorado Bureau of Investigation and, uh, we're assisting the Frederick Police Department with this case involving, uh, Chris Watts. And this is Tim Martinez...

Q1: Also an agent for CBI.

Q: Sir, if you'd just introduce yourself?

A1: Uh, Duane Kessinger. I'm Ni-Nichol's father.

Q: Duane, what's your birthday?

A1: November 3, 1958.

Q: And home address for you, sir?

A1: West 65th Avenue.

Q: What city?

A1: And that's, uh, Arvada, 80004.

Q: And a cell phone or, uh, home phone or where - on we can reach you?

A1: Um, it's 720-982-4547.

Q: Thank you. And Nichol can you just introduce yourself for the recording?

A: Nichol Kessinger. Do you need all the other stuff too?

Q: Yes, please.

A: I live at, um, 12255 Claude Court, Unit #612. Phone number is 720-656-9605.

Q: Claude Court, is that - I think we determined it was Northglenn, right?

A: Yes.

Q: Do you know your zip code?

A: 80241.

Q: Okay. Can you speak up just a little bit so the recorder...

A: Yeah.

Q: I know you're tired and you're stressed, um, and we won't be here any longer than we have to be. Uh, you've already had a conversation with people before. You came here on your own free will to talk to us, we picked you up at - at your request and brought you here. Um, you can get up and leave at any time. You don't have to talk to us. If there's a question you don't want to answer don't answer it. If you don't want to talk anymore just tell me I want to - I - tell me, "I want to leave," and I'm kind of in the way of the door but you're not being - uh, you're - you're not being, uh, interrogated as a criminal suspect, we're here to understand, uh, your relationship with Chris and what you know about Chris and his family and, uh, events relating to Chris Watts. Um, and do you know him as Chris or Christopher?

A: Either one.

Q: Okay. Um, so the phone number that you reached him on, can you tell me what that number was?

A: I think I deleted that out of my phone too. I just like cut him out of my life. It's a 910 number, you guys have it.

A1: Well, we gave it to (Mark) yesterday.

A: Yeah. So...

Q: I - I probably have it, but just in case...

A: ...he'll have it. I don't have it anymore.

Q: If I recited it to you, would you know it?

A: Just the first three numbers.

Q: Okay. But you...

A: 91...

Q: ...know it as a 910 number?

A: Yes that's what I do know. I - I mean, that's...

Q: Okay.

A: ...what I've got.

A1: North Carolina or something.

Q: Yeah North Carolina.

A: That's what it is.

Q: Okay. So let's just start, uh, with like a timeline of your, um, getting to know Chris, how you guys met, where you met, all those things. Let's just run - and I- I'm not gonna ask you specific questions unless I think it's necessary, I'll let you just tell me your story. I think it's a little bit easier that way. So I just want to know how you met him, where you met him, how long you guys were dating, uh, and those kind of things initially.

A: Okay. Um, I think I met him sometime in June, probably early June it might've been May, it was just talking at work, it was pretty casual. Um, and, uh, he didn't have a wedding ring on his finger and every time I talked to him he didn't tell me that he was in a relationship, he didn't even mention his kids right away either. Um, and then one day he told me that he had two kids, I was like that's pretty cool. And, uh, so he was telling me about his kids...

Q: That sounded like a sarcastic comment.

A: No I thought it was kind of cute, I was like oh he's a dad. It was like right around Father's Day too so whenever that is, is that in June? Yeah.

Q: Okay. I'm not good with holidays.

A: So that's - he told me he had kids and then it was Father's Day shortly after that so...

Q: Okay.

A: ...that's what I do know. And I was like - no, I thought it was cute. And then, um, he was telling me about 'em, he was pretty excited about 'em. And then, um, he mentioned that he did have a significant other, and then he told me that those two were in the process of a separation.

Q: Did he mention the children's name or his significant other's name?

A: Um, I didn't know his significant other's name for a while. And then I think he told me his kids' names pretty quick but to be honest with you on an exact date of when that happened I don't know.

Q: So in May and June - first of all, where do you work?

A: I work at Anadarko Petroleum Corporation. I'm contracted to Anadarko Petroleum Corporation.

Q: Okay, and you work out of an office setting where?

A: In Platteville, Colorado.

Q: Okay. And Chris also works out of that location, per se?

A: Yes. Yes. He's in the field, but he comes into the office with his team.

Q: So you work - uh, what is your job responsibility?

A: I do healthy- health, safety, and environment.

Q: Okay. So you work in the office, and you take care of health safety for - Anadarko is an oil and gas company, right?

A: Yes.

Q: So you're doing health safety in the office and Chris works in the field...

A: Yes.

Q: ...as a - what - what kind of job does he do?

A: He's an operator so I don't know like all of his daily duties but he's a field operator so he works with like the oil wells.

Q: So he goes out and does work on those whatever...

A: Yes.

Q: ...uh, that work might be. But he comes into the office frequent for...

A: In the mornings. His team meets in the mornings, they don't - they're not all in there every day. Some days some of 'em are in there, some days other one are in there but in the mornings typically from like 6:15 to probably 7:00, somewhere around there.

Q: And is that where you met Chris?

A: Yes.

Q: Okay. So can you just take us through kind of a little bit of, uh, the early part of how you guys - how he courted you or you courted him, I don't know which one happened, um, how you guys got to know each other?

A: Um, I guess we just started talking, he actually - um, so part of my job is to manage the gas monitors that we have so Anadarko requires all of their field personnel to carry like, uh, gas monitor sensors for toxic gases and it's my job to control all the inventory, any issues, anything like that. Um, and we were havin' some pretty serious like equipment issues and we had, uh, numerous amounts of people coming in my office one day and he happened to be one of them. Um, and I had seen him before, like they meet in the - in the lunchroom and that's where I go put my lunch in the fridge so I had seen him but I didn't never like talk to him. Um, so that day we just started talking and then every time I saw him in the hallway after that and it was always hit or miss, like it wasn't an everyday thing, it was just when I saw him we just started talking and we just kind of had a lot in common and just hit it off so we'd always have, you know, pretty good conversations. And then I don't know, one day he just - he - he told me that he had kids and started talking about his kids and then mentioned, "Yes that I have a wife but we're getting separated." I said, "Okay," and then...

Q: When do you think that was?

A: When he said all that?

Q: So specifically when he told you he was getting separated from his wife, was that within the first couple weeks that you knew him, or was that later on? You said you met him around May or June...

A: Yeah, it was still in June.

Q: Okay.

A: It would've been before Father's Day.

Q: So had you guys ever gone out on any kind of, um…

A: No.

Q: …date at that time? You just were…

A: No, no, no, no.

Q: …conversing at work?

A: Yeah, that's all it was. And then, um, I don't know, we started hanging out. We hung out, we went to - we went to a park, hung out at a park.

Q: Let's go back real quick, so he took - why did he tell you that he was getting a divorce? Did he ask you out at that time?

A: No, he didn't. I think he was probably interested in me and so, um, he talked to me a couple times, uh, via his work phone and I was like, uh, no. Like it was still very like friendly conversation. But then when I realized like this man is interested in me, I'm interested in him, this is personal, so we got away from the Anadarko thing 'cause I really don't want those guys affiliated with any of this. And…

Q: So you have a work phone that's specifically…

A: No. I have one phone that I do both on. He has two phones.

Q: Okay. So he had your phone, the 720-656…

A: That's the only number that I wrote with all the time.

Q: Okay.

A: So he has two phones.

Q: All right. And one of those owned by Anadarko and...

A: Yes, sir.

Q: ...one personal.

A: Yes, sir.

Q: Do you know what his Anadarko phone number was?

A: Nope.

Q: Okay.

A: It's been so long and I mean I'm sure I could like look it up but I tried to look it up for those guys yesterday and I couldn't find it.

Q: Okay.

A: Um...

Q: We can find it, that's okay. I just wondered if you knew it.

A: Um, but at that point we just like took it to his phone 'cause I just felt it was like better that way. Um, and we just continued to talk and then, um...

Q: Let me go back to the park, where was the park?

A: It's like down the street from my house, it's called East Lake #3.

Q: Your - your house...

A: Yes.

Q: ...in Northglenn?

A: Yes.

Q: And that was in the June timeframe?

A: I - yeah. Well like the beginning of July, it was like right around my birthday like so sometime in the very end of June, beginning of July.

Q: Okay. And that's the first meeting you had outside of work?

A: Yeah.

Q: Um, basic conversation for a first date?

A: I mean we kept it pretty simple I guess, you know, um, I don't even remember everything we talked about...

Q: Sure.

A: ...we were there for a few hours, um, but...

Q: Understand my - so if - if I ask about conversation what I'm looking for was he talking about his family during any of these meetings? Those are the kind of - I understand, uh, there- you know, whatever you guys were talking about relationship, your life, your interest, those things, I - we don't need to know that. What I'm interested in is knowing is when he brings up his children, when he brings up his wife, when he brings up financial information, when he brings up his home, when he brings up anything that may have been - and - and it's been a few days so you've had a chance to reflect on, um, some articles that you may have read and you know unfortunately that you're in a situation where somebody has been murdered. And that information when you look backwards, um, in your memory what the conversations with Chris anything that he might've said that would be relative to that - and I'm not just, you know, and even if one day he was mad and he said I want to do this or do that, um, you know, anything like that, if he ever made any kind of statements that you were like whoa that was weird, um, or why would he say that or why did he mention that. Do you understand what I'm - I'm looking for?

A: No I completely understand, I just feel like some of this happened so long ago that I can't tell you like the exact words of the exact conversation at the exact time and place...

Q: Sure.

A: ...because it's like we had a lot of conversations. I mean we talked every single day so it's like...

Q: So if there's a...

A: ...I'm trying to help you guys with the stuff like the stuff that's more current I can give you guys a lot more like detail and exact times but when you're asking me about something that happened six weeks ago and exactly what was said it's like - I mean I'm sure I can give you a general idea but to be honest with you like to pinpoint exact words it's not gonna happen.

Q: I'm not lookin' for exact words, um, just more - let's say six weeks ago he said something that triggered with you last night, um, that's what I'd be looking for. Or something four weeks ago. And if you don't remember where it was or the specific words that doesn't matter, just he said something that was off the wall or he said this or he said that, that has caused you a moment to pause and you go wow I wonder why he said that, now knowing what you know today. Do you understand where - where I'm goin' with that.

A: I completely understand and to be honest with you I mean there were several discussions that we had about his current relationship and where it had gone and what it had caused, um, and he talked about his kids from time to time. But the thing was is was never hostile, it was never anything aggressive. Like even when he spoke of his wife and the fact that they were separating it was never like ill, it was - it was very - it was still very kind, it was just like, "This is not working," you know, and would explain why but it wasn't anything out of the ordinary or anything that I think would scare me. And to this day even after everything that I found out I still look back at that and I don't see any red lights with the way that he spoke of his family.

Q: Okay.

A: At all.

Q: Can you just describe his de- overall demeanor over the 8, 10, 12 weeks that you guys knew each other?

A: It wasn't that long, it was like six weeks that we were hangin' out. Well I guess we knew each other longer but...

Q: Okay but you met him in the office and just his overall persona of who was - was he aggressive, was he mellow, was he calm, was he outspoken? Well who was Chris?

A: He - I, you know, I think he's an introvert, I would consider him to be like a pretty - I don't want to say he's a very reserved individual, I think he's probably more reserved around other people. I think he emphasized to me that one of the reasons that he really enjoyed talking to me is because if - he felt like he could get out of his shell. He said around most people he just like didn't really feel the - the need to - to like talk and converse. And it wasn't just in his home life, just in general it wasn't something where he - he's an introvert. And he said with him - with me it made him feel like he could really just start talking about things that excited him and I think a lot of that had to do with the fact that we had things in common. Um, so with me I think he was a little bit more outgoing but even then I would still consider him to be an introvert. I mean not...

Q: So...

A: ...on the extreme end. If an introvert went to like 1 to 10 I'd put him at like a 4 or a 5, so on the lighter side of introversion.

Q: ...so pretty even keel?

A: Yes like really relaxed like all the time, he was never really like worked up about anything. Just...

Q: Mellow...

A: ...chilled.

Q: ...easy-going guy.

A: Very much.

Q: Okay. And he was that way with you - did you ever - did he ever have any kind of, uh - did you guys ever have arguments? I mean...

A: No.

Q: ...pretty short relationship, no arguments during that time?

A: No.

Q: Did he ever lose his temper at any time?

A: Never.

Q: You guys never had a yelling match?

A: No.

Q: So you never saw him upset or mad?

A: No. And there was a couple times that we had some disagreements on some things that as we like further progressed into this story, you know, but it was never - like I am very calm when I talk to people, it's like extremely rational when I handle situations that there's a disagreement in and he always was the exact same way, like always. Like I never stress anything. I think one thing that actually kind of drew me to him was the fact that he was like very open with communicating with me if there were any like differences on how we saw things or - or just like open-minded about things. It was - it was - actually I - I personally thought it was kind of unique because usually most of the men that I've ever met are typically very closed off and I didn't get that from him at all. But it was always like kind. Very kind.

Q: So no sense that this guy had a temper or...

A: Not at all.

Q: ...wasn't - was aggressive or he never lost his mind and yelled and said crazy stuff or anything like that?

A: No.

Q: Okay.

A: No.

Q: So can we just kind of go back to your relationship, you say you guys had a lot in common. What - what was that?

A: Well I mean like were both really into fitness, I think that's important, it's a lifestyle. Um, both of us ate pretty healthy so I think that was important as well. Um, he is like a total gearhead, he likes cars a lot and I don't know nearly as much about them but it's always been something that I've been pretty interested in so we'd definitely talk about stuff like that. Um, and I guess he was always willing to like learn new stuff, and vice versa. Like I like to travel a lot, it's not something that he's done a lot but he seemed like really interested in what I had to share with him and vice versa. So even if it wasn't something that we originally had in common together it was just like hey I respect what you have to say, and vice versa.

Q: So you guys just yin and yang, you got along pretty well?

A: Very well.

Q: And no time he never gave you any indication that…

A: None.

Q: …that he was having issues, um, so you - when - during your guys' dating time did you guys spend most of the time at your place?

A: Always.

Q: Okay. Always at your place.

A: I told - well or we'd go out but, um, I told (Mark) yesterday, he asked me if I went over there and I told him about one time that I went over to that house. I've been to that house twice but it was very, very brief and it was not like an extended stay. I did not feel comfortable there or like I just didn't want to be there, it's not my life, like that is somebody else's life and somebody else's existence and I respect that, that's their space. So I used to tell him, "Well come to my house because this is - like this is our space, this is my space." And so for me out of respect just for like whatever situation he had going on and the fact that it's not my home, um, I felt that it was better to - to be in my place. And I - I live alone, I don't have any roommates or anything so it's pretty easy to do that.

Q: So during June and July did you - were you aware that he, uh - his family was not - his - did you meet his children…

A: No…

Q: …during June and July?

A: …I didn't want to. And he didn't ask me to.

Q: Okay.

A: I mean not that I didn't want to ever, it was just not now, it's like you're not finalized with your separation and not only that, we've barely been dating, like you can't introduce kids to somebody new in a situation like that, that's something that takes time. I mean would I have liked to have met them, of course. They, you know, I mean that would've been a - a great honor for me to have somebody introduce their children into my life, you know, and - and - but not then. It was something that it was like okay well let's see where we're at in six months, let's see where we're at in a year and if we're still doing this and you and me are still, you know, happy with where we're at and you think that this is something that is gonna be long term and is worth bringing your children into the picture then yes I would love to meet them. But it's like not right now. You are still in this situation when you're not even completely out of it and I'm getting in it and that's not fair for them. And that was kind of the policy that I had with him was it was just like yes but not yet.

Q: So did he ask to introduce you to his children?

A: Not at that time.

Q: Okay.

A: I think both him and I were on the same page of eventually if things went as they should in a relationship…

Q: I understand you guys' relationship is very new and young and, um…

A: Yeah.

Q: …so although it was short I - just laying everything out helps us understand what actually was going on with him and..

A: Yeah.

Q: ...some - we may - I might as her a question and you're going why the heck would he ask her that, probably because I have information that I'm not willing to share with you and I'll tell you that right now. I'm not gonna tell you - some questions I'm gonna ask you and you'll go, "What the heck?" I won't - I won't share some information with you, just it protects you and it protects our investigation so if it seems weird there's a reason I'm asking it and...

A: That's fine.

Q: ...it's usually relative to what I know. Um, so don't - don't take offense to it, again it's just part of what we need to know. Um...

A: Understood.

Q: So just - you went to his house on two occasions...

A: Yes.

Q: ...were - was that recent?

A: No that was like pretty early into it and I did not like it and did not want to go back.

Q: Do you recall where the house was?

A: Yeah it's like right off the highway in Frederick.

Q: Okay. And you know the streets?

A: I mean I'm sure I could figure it out again if I like really had to, like off the top of my head no.

Q: Do you know the street name?

A: No.

Q: Okay.

A: I would have to like drive around in there to get there.

Q: Okay. Um, did it look like anybody else lived at that house at that time?

A: Oh definitely.

Q: Okay.

A: I mean the whole thing...

Q: So is that what freaked you out?

A: I mean he told me that he was living in the basement, um, and said, "We're separated but we're not divorced and we're gonna get ready to sell the house." And that was the impression that I was under. And I was under the impression that they were taking everything pretty slow with this with like getting ready to sell the house, I mean those are big things. So that's what I was informed and I mean if you think about it this whole thing happened in a six week stretch, like that's really that much of a timeframe. So in that sense like its believable to me. Um, yes I went - I went to the house and, um, the first time I was there, um, I hung out in their like front living room, I just sat on the floor and it was on the 4th of July, it was the morning of the 4th and I was helping him, uh, to set up My Fitness Pal app and like track his food and his calories and stuff 'cause he does pretty good with the working out and stuff and he asked me, he's like, "Can you help me just like get this dialed in?" I was like, "Yeah I can do that." So that - he invited me up to the house and I was already kind of hesitant to do it 'cause I was like there are other people that live here I just felt like it was an invasion of space. And so I went up there and we just stayed in that front room and I helped him out with that, um, and got him all set up with that. And then, uh, oh he asked me if I wanted lunch and he grilled chicken and carrots. Chicken and carrots. And then, uh, that's all he had and I was like okay. So we, uh, so we ate and then I left. And then there was another day about - I can give you the date ish, let me look at a calendar. I think it was the weekend after my birthday.

A1: Um, just a thing on the courtesy for the phone for - what was that guy's name, (Don)?

Q: This gentleman...

A: Oh.

Q: ...(unintelligible). I just met him today.

A: Um...

Q: Do you want to do the phone...

A: ...I forgot about that.

A1: For TPD?

Q: It's not for them, they're doing it for us.

A1: Yes.

Q: We just didn't - we don't have the equipment with us to do it and I asked them to do it for us. They're not involved in this investigation. He would just be a, uh, computer person. He would not be looking at any of this stuff. That, uh, would fall to myself. So keep that in mind, he's not involved in this investigation. Thornton PD has nothing to do with this other than lettin' us use their facility and, um, helping us with some electronic download. He's not gonna look at your phone right now. He's gonna put it on a disk and they're gonna give it to me.

A: Gotcha. I don't know, what do you think? I really want to help you guys, I do.

A1: It's up to you.

A: I feel like I'm - I'm - this whole thing is just gonna be crazy regardless of whether I give you my phone or not. I mean that's kind of how I look at it, like it's happening, it's gonna happen.

A1: Well the texts reiterate what you've been...

A: The media is just gonna...

A1: ...saying all along so it's not like...

A: Well they do, that's the only thing too. I mean that's kind of a good backup. Yeah I'll give it to 'em.

Q: I think you hit the nail right on the head. There is reasons why we want everything. Um, it validates things that we know. I'm not gonna come out and tell you that I - if you tell me something today we'll validate it with your text messages. Whether it's the ones we have now...

A: Yeah. Yeah, yeah. I will...

Q: ...or the ones you're gonna give us. Certainly.

A: I'll give it to 'em. If you want to go get him - I was...

Q: I want you to read this is what I want you to do before you decide that, okay? Um...

A: So the second time I went to the house I'm not sure what day it was but it was the weekend of the 14th.

Q: On - of August?

A: July.

Q: July.

A: I don't know if it was the 14th or the 15th, um, one of those two days. But we had went out and we stopped there just real quick on the way back. And we were there not very long but that time I saw a picture of his wife and one of his kids. And I remember thinkin' to myself like wow she's so beautiful, and I like took a step back and I was just like this man has a gorgeous house, he has beautiful babies, he has a beautiful wife, he has an awesome job, like why would he want to leave this? And I remember talking to him about it and that was the first time that I tried to actually say, "What do you think about not separating from your li- wife? Like what if you really try to work on this?" And he had expressed to me that, "We've tried to work on this and it's not working so that is why we're separating." And I spent some time like just, you know, kind of - 'cause it - it almost made me feel bad where I was like to the point where I'm engaging in a relationship with a man who the way he described it is in a contractual agreement but was not in like an emotional relationship with somebody. Um, and for me the way I would have preferred to do this is to avoid it 'til that contractual agreement was also done and he was done. And he could've approached me and said, "I'm - just had a divorce, you know, maybe we could take this slow. What do you think?" But instead it was, "Oh we're separated and we're working on a divorce," and that is the part that I feel bad about because I should've waited on that and I didn't. And, you know, I was just like well they're already there so, you know, but then being in that house I was just like, "Why? Fix this. Find a way to fix this, make it work," you know, and I would - I would - I was like trying to push him to do it and he seemed pretty reluctant to do it, he didn't want to. And, um, I don't know, we were still seeing each other fairly frequently but I kind of like backed away so we weren't hangin' out quite as much and we were still close but it was just like I really wanted him to try, like I wanted to know that he tried and it didn't work and then he moved on, not that, you know, they both kind of tried and then he got himself into a situation with somebody else. And I don't know - I just thought he had a beautiful life goin' on and he cold have made it work. That was the way I looked at it from the outside.

Q: So is this something you reflected on since this event or was this you...

A: No I was doing it then, like you can see it in my...

Q: You said this - this doesn't look right, he's kind of, um - I don't want to be responsible for breakin' up a marriage, especially with two children, is that kind of the gist I'm gettin' here?

A: I didn't think it didn't look right, I mean I - I think he was legitimately sleeping in the basement and I don't - I didn't think that these two were - I mean I think it was like hey we're both stuck in this house for now, we gotta sell this, in the meantime you live here, I live here, we sleep in different rooms, take care of the kids. That's just like kind of...

Q: Okay.

A: ...how I took that. And, um, no I didn't think it didn't look right, I just thought it just seemed like he had so much going on and it was just beautiful that it was like, "Why don't you just try this out, you know, and see if you can fix it." And he'd always be like, "Well what about us? What about us?" I'm like, "Don't worry about us. Like that is more important. Like try to see if you can like salvage whatever it is that you have going on with your wife," and - and, you know, he - I always got the impression that he was a great father to his kids, like always. And so, you know, and I was like, "And be the dad that you want to be," I was like, "And see if you can make it work." And he just - like we kind of talked about it off and on for like a few weeks and I was just kind of like I don't know, like I think I was kind of like cold feetin' about it when I went - after I went over to his house. And so this was like pretty early on. And then, um, he told me that, uh, oh he went to, um - he went to North Carolina and he was like, "I'm gonna talk to her when I'm in North Carolina and see if I can get her to do this, to like try to like rekindle the flame."

Q: Okay so try to, uh, salvage his relationship as you've been asking him to do?

A: Yes. And - and then if he decided...

Q: When did he go to North Carolina?

A: Um, I think it was like the last week of July, somewhere around there.

Q: Okay.

A: So I mean this was like a couple weeks that I was just kind of like trying to push him to do that.

Q: So let's - let's pause that North Carolina and we'll come...

A: Okay.

Q: ...back to that real quick. I want you to read this. If you don't understand what it means than ask me the question. But basically what it says is you have the right not to let me look at your phone. I am asking to look at your phone for the purposes we previously discussed for the text messages and your phone log and unfortunately the photos that are attached therein too. Um, that information is only rel- relative to this investigation, I'm not lookin' at anything else except for the conversations between you and Chris Watts, and the phone, um, data between you and Chris Watts for phone calls for times and dates for those phone calls. Um, and then the content of the text messages that - that are there. And we can - we'll write that specifically down here, understand that if...

A: I just don't want anybody to get some of those texts, like they have nothing to do with this case and they are just like...

Q: Between you and Chris?

A: Yes they're just - they're just...

Q: So just tell me what you're...

A: They're just kind of raunchy.

Q: Okay well...

A: Like I don't need anybody - I don't need that...

Q: Everybody's an adult...

A: ...posted like...

Q: We're not gonna post it.

A: ...somewhere.

Q: Um, it - the...

A: I don't need...

Q: ...the only ones that...

A: ...I don't want the newspapers to get that, that's all I want.

Q: The only ones that...

A: I just need them to not get that.

Q: ...we would be looking for, again, is the same kind of questions we're getting to here is things about his children, things about his wife...

A: Understood. Understood.

Q: ...that the questioning of did he ever, you know, has he ever said something to you that might indicate maybe not then but now that there was something like this in his mind. Or you - you know what we're lookin' for, I don't need to come out and tell you that. I understand the embarrassment of particular photos or potential, um, sexual types of conversations you may have had with Chris, uh, it's - it's not relative to - to the investigation we don't care, okay? You're an adult, I'm an adult, everybody in this room's a- even your dad and I give it to you for saying that stuff in front of your dad 'cause I'm not sure many women could do that. Um, so that's not what we're - we're after. We're after the - the information that corroborates things that you've told us and also that corroborates or, um, may tend to prove that things that Chris told us were a lie. You understand that?

A: Mm-hm.

Q: Um, and that's maybe going a little bit far, I usually won't tell people that but because of your reservations that's what I'm lookin' for. If I can disprove something he's told me by a phone record, phone records don't lie, people do. Okay? So if I can disprove something that may be important that's what I need it for. I'm not saying I can, has it happened before? Absolutely. Is it critical in cases that I've worked in the past? Yes. So that's why I want it. Okay? Um, again, you don't have to give it to me, you can tell me, "I don't want you to have it, go get a warrant," um, I'm not even gonna tell you if I go get a war- try to get a warrant right now. I'm just asking for you to consent and - and again we can write right here what you're willing to give me which is the text messages and the phone log and unfortunately again the - the attachments on some of those text messages. And I'll write it on there and then you'll just sign it, okay? Do you under- do you understand the questions there? Do you have questions about any of the things that it says? You understand you don't have to do this…

A: Mm-hm.

Q: …you're doing it of your own free will? And I know you're tired so if you want to let your dad read it too, um…

A: He will, thank you.

Q: …that's - that's a good idea.

A: Can you fill it out before I sign it?

Q: Yep. And just you read it and if you have any questions then we'll - we'll put on there what we're after.

A: I'm so hungry.

Q: You should've told me, I would have got you some food. I got food in my car.

A: It's not staying down, it's coming up…

A1: She hadn't been feelin' good. Not 'cause of any - just…

A: Like I got sick prior to this…

A1: The gym.

A: …whole - whole thing happening, and then I think ev- all of this compounding with the fact…

Q: Stress.

A: …that I'm sick it's just not good. I have not really been eating or sleeping much at all.

A1: Yeah I - I am with you, we - we definitely need to accelerate the case because the more lo- the more it takes the less sure that they are of situations. But on the other end I think if we - if you do just that only…

Q: You tell me what you're willing to provide to me and we'll write it on…

A1: I- is that good enough?

A: Mm-hm. I just want like our text conversation and then our phone call records.

Q: So I'm gonna put, um...

A: So the time and date of the phone call records and then our text message on those.

Q: Text...

Q1: Could we get photos of him?

A: Huh?

Q1: Could we get photos of him?

A: Off of that?

Q1: Would you mind if we got his photos that he sent to you?

A: Well they'll be in that text message thing.

Q: So all of his photos were sent - there was no apps or anything else...

A: No. No, no, no, no, no.

Q: ...you used that you guys were sending?

A: No.

Q: It was all just text messages?

A: Yeah.

Q: Okay. So it'd be an attachment to a text that he sent you?

A: Pretty much.

Q: But...

A: Ev- everything is in the text and the phone call records.

Q: So...

A: Like all of it.

Q: ...because we don't have it on tape, we discussed prior to turning the tape on, um, on Tuesday which would've been the 14th of August, um, you had read some newspapers articles on the 13th and the 14th that regarded this case, you had also had a conversation with Chris at some point during the day on Monday, uh, and on Tuesday because of what you found, specifically what you said was - and don't let me put words in your mouth but you kn- you found out that his, um, wife was pregnant.

A: And I - yes.

Q: And you did not know that prior?

A: No.

Q: And you found that out via the newspaper articles and that caused you concern. Um...

A: Well I just realized that he was lying to me and I was like, "Well if you can lie to me about this what else are you lying to me about?" And it made me realize that maybe his wife was in danger at that point and it was Day 2 too and she still wasn't home.

Q: What did that cause you to do with your phone though?

A: Oh, what, when I deleted those? I was just kind of grossed out by him to be honest with you. I was just like, "I don't know what's going on right now but you just lied to me and I don't want to see this come over my phone anymore." So I removed it.

Q: So you re- just - you already said, but you removed text messages?

A: I deleted all of his stuff because he lied to me. I mean that's what it was, it was hur- it was the hurt that made me delete it. And then it was the lie that made me start questioning everything else he had been telling me for the last few days.

Q: And that's when you decided to come forward?

A: Yes.

Q: Okay. So just for context...

A: Yes.

Q: ...when people delete stuff off phones usually we go hold on a second...

A: No, no, no, no, no it wasn't malicious at all.

Q: And - and - and that's why I want to (unintelligible)...

A: It wasn't malicious at all.

Q: ...and no I'm not saying it was malicious.

A: He - he - he lied to me, it just hurt. Like I had never felt like he had ever lied to me before and it was a big lie...

Q: Right.

A: ...I mean telling somebody that you're in the midst of a divorce and then you have a wife that has a 15 week old baby on the way is a huge, huge thing and I was very taken back and I was just - it was hurt. And so at that point I just - I like deleted it. I had a - I had a few more quick things to say to him and then I just got rid of him. That's literally what I did, I just cut him out of my life. It would have honestly been like a bad breakup kind of thing. Like if none of this other stuff would have happened that's what it would have been, that would have been the end of it.

Q: The information was not destroyed because there was anything in there that would be, uh, harmful to you or potentially to Chris at this point, but harmful to you in particular, that's not what you did?

A: No. No, no, no, no, no.

Q: You did it out of -- uh, excuse my language -- this guy's an asshole so I'm gettin' rid of him and I'm gettin' this stuff off my phone.

A: That was like me kicking him out of my life.

Q: Okay.

A: And then - like I said and then realizing that he lied, that was when I was like okay maybe his family is in danger and they're not coming back and they're not staying with a friend.

A1: Yeah when'd I go over there? Tuesday morning?

A: Wednesday morning.

A1: Wednesday, yeah.

A: I called you Wednesday morning.

A1: That's when we started discussing you guys need to get everything that - I just...

Q: You can understand the importance of...

A1: Oh no question. We were...

Q: Like I said, people lie, phone records don't. Um, and they really help specifically, um, establish dates and times.

A: Mm-hm.

Q: I think we have a - have a very good grip on that in this case already but there may be a time when we go, "We need to know something else," and then we would have it, we don't want to lose it. And that's - that's really what it is for us is if we lose information that later on we go, "Man I wish we would've got that," and we may never even use these. We may never even look at 'em but if - if we have it now then we don't worry about losing it. So I appreciate you being cooperative and giving it to us.

A: Yeah.

Q: So the first thing I wrote was text messages between Chris Watts and attachments. Okay so 'cause we're talking about the photographs unfortunately that caused you much disdain. And then I am gonna put, uh, phone log for calls between, uh, yourself and Chris Watts. Your phone number is, uh...

A: 720...

Q: ...720...

A: ...656-9605.

Q: And this right now is located at - we're at the Thornton Police Department, it's gonna be moved to my - so this is kind of - doesn't make sense but we're here, it's gonna be moved to the Colorado Bureau of Investigation. He's gonna download it here but I'm gonna take it with me, just so you know, it's not staying here.

A: Okay.

Q: They're not gonna retain any of this, this comes with me.

A: Okay.

Q: Okay.

A1: Is there anything else you want on there? I think that's about...

A: That's it. I mean I don't have social media, I don't really have anything else you guys can pull.

Q: Okay.

Q1: Is there anything else you know of that could help us with this that we - that is not on this sheet?

A: Uh, as far as like data?

Q1: That's on your phone.

A: No. No I mean everything we did was like text and talk pretty much. I mean and like I said, any pictures that I had like even if you were to restore all my regular photos there's so many pictures in there and you wouldn't even know which ones were for him and which ones weren't. But the one - any picture that I wanted to send to him I sent via text so if you guys go through the text in the attachments you will have - you will have everything that wasn't said verbally and was done via text. But I think that's it, like I don't have - I don't have anything else as far as like no Facebook, no Instagram, no - no Twitter, no LinkedIn, like none of it. So, um, there was never any of that kind of correspondence. So I think that should probably cover everything you guys will need.

Q: Is there any particular messages that I - would help me so I don't have to look at - 'cause whatever is on your phone I don't know how long we're gonna get back to but let's say there - is there a particular date or time or message that stands out to you that would be relative to - specifically to the investigation into this case that might assist me in understanding why something like this could have occurred?

A: I'm still in shock that this whole thing happened, I...

Q: I can imagine.

A: ...I - like that's why I gave him the benefit of the doubt for the first day 'cause I was just like no way. Like I didn't even think about that, I mean murder was not on the top of my mind when somebody doesn't come home for an evening. Especially if they just like had some sort of like heated conversation, it's like okay you guys are separating, you have a heated conversation, you leave for a night, like I didn't even think this guy killed his wife. I mean that - that like - murder is not something on the top of my mind when I call one of my friends for three or four hours and she doesn't answer the phone. Like that doesn't even process to me as like a real thing that is a possibility at that point. And so that's why I gave it a day and then the second day I was talkin' to him he was just like a hot mess I could tell. And then with like the way he was talking to me and then that's kind of when I cut him off and I stopped talking to him. And then...

Q: So remember what you just said and we're gonna get to that 'cause that's probably a very important conversation. So but...

A: Yeah. So if you want to know days I would probably honestly just start at like Sunday and work your way forward. I mean all the rest of that stuff it's just like the small talk of like hey this, this, this, you know. I mean...

Q: And your relationship building through the first weeks...

A: Yeah I mean like and if you go like maybe like a week further back like there's times like I was trying to help him find an apartment like just for him, not for me, but for him and his kids, um, to get set up. And like there's times where I'm like, "Well where's your wife moving to? Like how close is she gonna be to you? You should be within like

30 minutes of your kids so they're close. And you want to be close to their school and close to your gym. And like what's your price range?" Like I was helping him get all of this stuff set up and it was like in a very decent manner and I don't know if all of that is in text, some of it's probably on the phone. Like at this point I've talked to him so much that I don't even know which parts are like verbalized and which parts are texted at this point...

Q: Right.

A: ...but we can figure it out.

Q: Okay. The - you see what I wrote, uh, text messages between Chris Watts and attachments. Uh, and then the phone logs for calls between your phone number and Chris Watts. That's - those are the two things that we'll ask to be extracted from your phone. So if you're okay with that, if you...

A: Why does that say, "As removed, cell phone data"? Isn't that this?

Q: That is that and that's what he's gonna remove.

A: Oh.

Q: And then that officer is gonna fill that out.

A: Gotcha. What is the date? I don't even know what day it is.

Q: Today is the 16th.

A: And you want to add anything to this?

Q: If you give - get your phone we'll get him started.

A: Oh other than we - yeah we just - we wanted to give you everything but we also want to be protected in doing so, is more of the...

Q: Sure.

A: …was more of the thing. It- it's just…

Q: And when he's done we'll give you our copy of this.

Q1: Is there a password or anything like it - will it lock up after a period of time?

A: Yeah. Yeah, yeah. (Unintelligible).

Q1: That's his notes.

A1: And…

Q1: Make sure there's nothing written on the back. I'm just teasing.

A: There's not. I checked before I ripped it off. Okay.

Q: Let's go back to North Carolina.

A: Okay.

Q: He went to North Carolina and he was trying to rehab his marriage with his wife?

A: Uh, he said he was…

Q: Do you know her name at this point?

A: Yeah.

Q: Okay. Are you okay saying her name?

A: It's Shanann.

Q: All right. And do you know the children's' name?

A: Yes it's Bella and Celeste, (CiCi).

Q: She went by - they called her (CiCi)?

A: Mm-hm.

Q: All right. So he went to - were they in North Carolina already?

A: They were already there.

Q1: If you want something.

A: I don't know if my stomach will do that. Um, yeah they were already out there. He just flew out there to go meet up with…

Q: Do you know why they were there?

A: They're - they're all from there.

Q: Okay so they were - they're from…

A: They were visiting her family for the most part until he got there. And then they still were mostly visiting her family.

Q: Okay. And do you know how long they had been there?

A: A while, like weeks.

Q: All right. And he flew out to join his family there?

A: Yep.

Q: Do you know specifically where you flew to?

A: What airport?

Q: No, no, no, what city.

A: No not off the top of my head.

Q: Okay.

A: I'm sure if I thought real hard maybe I could think about it but I mean come up with it, no I don't know.

Q: All right. So he goes there, how - do you re- you said it was like the last week of July?

A: I think so, I think it was like one of the last days of July. I'm almost positive, I think it was a weekday.

Q: Okay.

A: Um, yeah he flew out there and I thought I had like convinced him to like try to make peace with her and I was like, "If you guys work on this like I'm out 'cause what's the point? Like I'm not trying to be with somebody that's in another relationship," which I know that sounds silly given the whole relationship that we had in the first place but I really was under the impression that they were separating. I mean it was like reiterated to me so many times that that's what I thought it was. And it made sense to me too because like he could pretty much call me whenever he wanted, like I was the one that would tell him like, "Hey when your kids are awake you need to spend time with your kids. Like do that. And then after they go to bed like if you want to talk to me you can talk to me." But it was never like this super, super restricted thing. Like sometimes like right after work if I was like still talking to him I'd get kind of bummed out and I'd, you know, I'd tell him, I'd just be like oh it's frustrating sometimes like having to like wait. But at the same time I was never like this is horrible or, you know, it was always like I understood why. But then once his kids were asleep he never like had any - it was like he could do what he wanted. Do you know what I'm saying? Like he was in...

Q: Sure.

A: ...his basement and she's upstairs and they're not speaking. So it kind of made sense, it wasn't like sneaky...

Q: And you guys are just texting and...

A: We're talking or whatever, you know...

Q: Sure.

A: ...I mean and it was just - it was like I said, it was at certain times but that ti and originally it wasn't but it was me that put that timeframe on there because I thought he should hang out with his kids. Um...

Q1: Those two times that you were at his house did you see any evidence of that, him living in the basement? Did he ever show you that area (unintelligible)?

A: I've seen it, yeah I went down there and saw his - his little workout equipment and there's a bed down there all set up, and the basement was all clean and organized and stuff so, um, like a - like a decent bed setup so it made sense to me like hey this is - this is what's happening down here. Um, so I saw it. Um...

Q1: Even though his family was in Nor- North Carolina for multiple weeks it appeared that he was still living in the basement?

A: Mm-hm.

Q1: Hm.

A: Well and he told me sometimes he would like go upstairs and sleep if - if like he was home alone 'cause I know she'd like go on business trips and stuff. But he's like, "I don't like that bed anyways," so he didn't really like to sleep up there. I was like okay. Um, even when it was just him. So that was the impression that I got. Um, I don't know what we were talking about, North Carolina?

Q: Let's - yeah go - go back to North Carolina.

A: So North Carolina. Um, so he still made very frequent communication with me when he was out there and at one point he told me that they sat down and they talked about it and he told her that he wanted to either fix things or - like to try to fix things and if she didn't want to fix them then they needed to like move forward with the separation and like actually file for a divorce at this point, was - was the impression that I got from this and just what he told me. And so, um, he said that she was like pretty receptive to like just not trying. He was like, "She seemed like she just wants me to go." He's like, "When she has her mind made up, she has her mind made up and that's what she want," and he's like, "She doesn't want to try anymore," and he's like, "And neither do I really." And he was like, "It's done," and he's like, um - and then the next day - I don't even know what days these were, some time when he was out there. He told me, um, "We're putting the house up for sale as soon as we get back." And I was like, "Whoa that was quick." And he was like, "It's her, she's ready to go." And I was like, "Okay." And so I left it at that and then, um, he got back and I started askin' him like, "What are you gonna do? Because the Colorado housing market is fire and you guys are gonna sell this house like real fast," and I'm like, "You need to start looking for new places to live." And I'm like, "Where do you want to live?" And I was really trying to help him out, I'm like, "Do you want to get a house? Do you want three bedrooms so you have one and each of your girls have one?" I'm like, "Do you want to, you know, like do you want an apartment? Like what do you want, you know, where do you want to live?" Because he's in Frederick but that whole area over there is just like a bunch of small towns and you can kind of just pick and choose, everything's kind of, you know, and so, um, he told me, "Well I like Brighton," and I was like, "Okay." And then he told me he wanted a two-bedroom apartment and he said he wanted one room for him and the other room for his two girls. And I thought it was kind of cute, like I remember telling him, I was like, "Yeah me and my sister had bunk beds like at my dad's house," and I was like, "When we were little girls." When we were - me and my sister are the same age apart as him and his - I mean as his two daughters, you know, so I told him, I was like, "They're gonna love it." I was like, "They might be like stuck in - in one room together," I was like, "But they'll become like best buddies." And it was really exciting, like I liked helping him and I just wanted him to like - I don't know. This is what he told me he wanted so I was like, "Well I will help you do the research." But another thing that I really took care of was to be like where is she moving to? I was never like, "You know what, screw your wife, try to get full custody," none of that bullshit. It was always just like, you know, I'd ask him, I'm like, "Well what kind of custody are you guys gonna have," 'cause he sa- he - at work they're about to switch his schedule so right now he's like a Monday through Friday and they're about to switch these guys to eight days on, six days off...

Q: Mm, that's tough.

A: That's awesome. And I - and I was - so I was tellin' - I was askin' him, I was like, "Are you gonna have your kids like on that set of days off?"

Q: Mm-hm.

A: I was like, "'Cause that would work perfect, like one week on, one week off," and I was just like, you know, we had just talked about it and I'm like, "What is your plan?" And he's like, "We haven't figured out exactly what we're gonna do about the kids yet," but he told me, he's like, "Colorado's a 50-50 state and she's okay with everything 50-50." Like he said that she was like on board with this because she wanted it too, like she was checked out of this relationship. So that was like how he made this sound, that it was like a very like kosher we're done kind of thing and...

Q: Did you ever give him like books or articles or anything to read about saving your marriage? Did you ever provide anything to him like that?

A: About saving his marriage?

Q: Yeah like how to recover a marriage or how to save a marriage or, you know, there's - there's all sorts of publications and books out there.

A: No. No but I did tell him - and I don't know if I did this through text or phone, that will be something you guys will I'm sure figure out. Um, but I would tell - I told him a few times like, "I think that you should take the time to read some articles, uh, about, um, what separation does to kids." You know, and I told him, I said, "When my parents separated we were literally like 3 and 5," we were almost the exact same age as these little girls. And I told him, I said, "You know, I was so young when it happened that it didn't really have like a big negative effect on me because I was so small that I really didn't process it too well." I was like, "But I do have cousins that their parents got divorced when they were like 10, 11, and I think that it hit 'em a little harder, you know," and I - and he's like, "Oh they'll be fine," you know, and I told em, I was like, "Even though they're small and you think that they'll be fine," I was like, "I think you guys should just read about it just so that you guys are prepared in case, yo know, one of these two starts having a hard time with the fact that you guys aren't in the same house anymore." You know, an- and - and I would tell him, I was like, "You know, there's pros and cons to it, like," 'cause he was like getting ready to do it and it would be like, you know, it's kind of cool havin' two Christmases and, you know, like your parents get to go, you know, be happy doing whatever it is they want to do with their lives and they don't have to be in a situation that's probably not good for the kids because it's not good for those two. You know, but at the same time it was like just read, like that's what I always used to tell him, I'd always tell him to like - I - I tell people to read about everything, reading is so good for you.

Q: So he at this time is telling you that yeah I am the guy trying to save the marriage and she doesn't want it?

A: That's what he told me. That's what he told me so…

Q: Okay.

A: ...um, and he - yeah and then he was like, "She doesn't want it so I'm not gonna do it." And then it was like, "We're filing for divorce, we're selling the house," and this was like all as soon as they were comin' back from North Carolina, like boom, boom, boom, boom, boom. And...

Q: Well do you recall when he gets back from North Carolina?

A: No. I don't even know how long he was out there, I know it was like less than two weeks and more than one.

Q: Okay.

A: I don't remember.

Q: So he's - he comes back early August, would that be fair?

A: Oh yeah, it was definitely like in the first two weeks somewhere.

Q: All right.

A: Probably the second week of August at some point. And then I don't remember when...

Q: Does his wife come back with him at that time or does he...

A: Yeah they all came back.

Q: They all come back at the same time.

A: They all came back. Um, and then, uh, yeah so he - he continues to just, you know, tell me that this is like what he wants and - and so I took the time - and you will see that in the text too where I like - like there - like I found this apartment, it was perfect, it was so cute, I was like, "It's in your price range, it's like 6 miles from the gym, it's 23 miles from work," I'm like, "You know, it's super close to Frederick, it's gonna be by your kids' school, like this is - this is the spot," you know, and - and - and I told him, I was like, "I'll keep looking for more places," and he's like, "Well there some that I want to go see too." And he actually had me thinking that he was gonna go look at these places this week before all this sh- stuff...

Q: Oh so this is fairly recent then if we're talking...

A: Oh this just happened like in the last couple weeks.

Q: He's gonna go look at apartments during...

A: He wanted me to go with him.

Q: When you say this week are you saying...

A: Like this - this week.

Q: ...Monday was the 13th...

A: Like this week.

Q: Okay.

A: Yeah so I told him, I was like, "Well pick out a few spots and if you want me to come with you I'll go look at 'em but you, you know..."

Q: You said earlier that he had never, um - or that the - the apartment wasn't for you and him, it was just for him and his children.

A: Oh yes.

Q: It wasn't - you weren't in- had no intentions of moving in with him?

A: No. I have my own spot, I still have a lease there 'til July, and even then like he never asked me to move in with him...

Q: Okay.

A: ...and I never tried to move in with him. I mean I told him - I mean I really tried to take everything with this whole situation very slow. The only part that I screwed up on was the fact that he wasn't completely separated from her when him and I decided to spend time with each other. That is where I screwed up. But other than that everything else it was always like, you know, you build your life, I'm gonna build my life, we will intertwine them but I am not ready to like do this. And he respected that and I - and I, um, I even said that and I don't know, I - that might be in the text but (unintelligible) that Chris like, "You need space, like you're just getting out of a divorce, like personally I think jumping into a new relationship is a little quick." I was like, "I was in a relationship earlier this year and I think this is also a little quick." And I'm like, "So why don't we take our time?" And I'm like, "If you guys end up doing a week on, a week off with your kids," I'm like, "The week you have your kids be with your children. And the week that you don't," I'm like, "I don't even want to see you every day," I'm like, "I think we should spend like a few days of that together," I'm like, "'Cause I like my space and I think you need your space, I think you need your space to like develop your identity again and like get it back," because I think he's just been like so wrapped up in this whole thing that he's got in his own life - in his life that he - I mean he doesn't remember probably what it's like to like be single or have time where it's like just him.

Q: Sure.

A: And so I was just like, you know, like embrace that. I think it's a beautiful thing and I really try to like take it smart with all that. And it was the same thing with his kids, I was just like, you know, like - and I - and we'd talk about things every once in a while where I - you know, I'd be like, "Hey if I ever meet," you know, 'cause like I have a lot of house plants is a good example, so I have a lot of house plants and I told - I told him, I was like, "One day if I ever meet your kids," I was like, "I'm gonna show these girls how to like paint pottery and plant some plants." I was like, "I think they would love to see something grow that they build, I think it would be really, really cute." And like little stuff like that but it wasn't very frequent, it wasn't, "Hey we should get married," and, "Hey we should have babies," and, "Hey I want to live with you," and, "Hey I need to meet your children now," and, "Let's cut the mom out," it was never like that.

Q: Okay. And that was - it - there was never any conversation about, you know, "We can't do this with her around, we can't do this with the kids around"?

A: Never.

Q: He never said that...

A: No.

Q: ...you never said that?

A: No. No.

Q: So there - there - the way you guys were trying to make this work was just, you know, slowly trying to come together because of his current situation and by your account your own...

A: Mine. I mean I don't want to rush.

Q: ...you're - you're just a - a independent person it sounds like pretty much.

A: Yeah.

Q: And, uh, but through text message or through conversation he never said, uh, "Hey, uh, you know, this is gonna be financial able - I'm not gonna be financially able to do this," or, "This isn't a good thing, I got these kids," none - none of those conversations ever came up?

A: No. I mean he told me like he had a budget restriction so for his apartment -- and I'm pretty sure this is in the text and this will probably be in the last couple weeks -- um, he told me $1100 to $1400 when I was asking him. Like 'cause I told him I'd help him do homework, I was like, "You do some homework, I'll do some homework, we'll knock this out because if you guys are for real putting the house up you gotta figure it out." Um, and so that was his budget and I remember asking him, I was like, "Are you sure you don't want to just get like a house?" And he's like, "I never thought about a house." I'm like, "Yeah you can rent houses man, like it's a thing," and he's just like, "I don't know if I can afford that." I was like, "Okay." And I knew that those two had been some financial trouble, I definitely found out a lot more about that situation in, uh, newspaper recently. Um...

Q: Okay so prior to the newspaper how did you know he was in financial difficulty?

A: 'Cause he - I mean I - when I went to that house everything in there is very, very, very, very nice, it looks like it all comes with a very expensive price tag. And, uh, I didn't say anything to him about it but I could kind of tell then where I was just looking at everything like how do you guys afford this. And then he has that car, that's - I don't even know how much that car costs but I bet its...

Q: What car - what car is that?

A: That Lexus. I'm sure that thing cost like 80 grand. But just like money, like everything just looked like it cost a lot of money in that house.

Q: You probably have a decent idea of how much money he makes.

A: Yeah and it's not enough money to pay for all that, not even close.

Q: And did you have any idea what, um, Shanann did for a living or how much money she might've made?

A: I mean I had an idea, I don't - I mean I would consider her like a sales rep, I don't know how else to describe that. Um, for the company that she worked for and, uh, I don't know exactly how much she made. He said that she was really competitive and she like to try to keep up with him. He's like, "She gets close sometimes." So I don't know how much those two brought in. I mean off the top of my head if I could guess, probably somewhere around like $140K a year. I mean I don't know. 'Cause I don't know exactly how much he makes and I don't know exactly how much she makes. But based just off of what I know about the oil field, like yeah I - I would say that's probably an accurate estimate.

Q: So he - even if they're makin' let's just use the figure $100,000, they're living above they're means or below their means?

A: Oh - oh my God, like...

Q: Way too much?

A: Way, way, way, way too...

Q: Did he ever discuss with you any of those issues?

A: I mean a little, I mean I didn't know about the bankruptcy or any of that 'til I read on the newspaper about that but he just - he - I think he was really frustrated with the situation. Um, he told me, he's like, "You know, I feel like my paycheck goes in my bank account and I just watch it go like this," he's like, "But it doesn't have to," he's like, "She makes it like that." And I was just like...

Q: So was he resentful for that?

A: I don't know if he was resentful, I just think he was frustrated by the fact that they could be doing a lot better financially and she -- from the vibe that I got -- had really bad spending habits.

Q: So she was a spender. Um, the car hers or his?

A: I think it's hers.

Q: Okay.

A: I'm pretty sure that that's hers.

Q: Do you know what other car they might have?

A: Well I mean his APC pickup truck.

Q: And that's - that...

A: That's it I think.

Q: ...and that's owned by Anadarko though, right?

A: Yeah.

Q: So...

A: But so I don't - I don't think they own any other vehicles as far as I know. I think it's just that thing.

Q: And - and - and Anadarko who doesn't allow him to drive that on his own personal, right?

A: No. No.

Q: So he's just got one vehicle...

A: Yeah.

Q: ...um, and it's a very expensive Lexus. Um, and then they live in a pretty expensive house, I...

A: It's a huge house.

Q: Yeah. Yeah.

A: I was very taken back, when I saw it I was just like whoa, how do you guys…

Q: And then the fixtures inside caused you to pause…

A: Everything. Everything was just like…

Q: And you mentioned today you read something about, uh, bankruptcy…

A: Yeah.

Q: …what did you read?

A: That those guys filed bankruptcy for a lot of money and…

Q: Who are those guys?

A: Two tho- that couple.

Q: Okay.

A: In 2015. Oh Shanann and Chris…

Q: Thanks.

A: …filed bankruptcy in 2015.

Q: Okay. And you said for a lot of money, do you recall the amount?

A: No because it was different in each of the newspapers and I don't know which one to believe so…

Q: Okay.

A: Hundreds of thousands of dollars. So, um, yeah I didn't know that.

Q: So let's go just back though, him and the financial, he tells you - or he has a concern enough to at least express some con- something to you that he's frustrated with the way she spends or he's upset with working so hard and never having any money and she's kind of the responsibility, she's the responsible party for spending most of the money?

A: I - I pretty much got that vibe. I mean he just told me, he's like, "We're house broke all the time." And I was just like, "That's unfortunate," and I asked him, I was like, "Do you have 401K," and he was like, "Yeah." And I mean the reason I ask him this is because if I get in a relationship with somebody I want to know like what kind of baggage that they have, I think that's important if I walk into a situation where I'm like hey I have good credit and I have all of these things that I've been building and you don't have your stuff together like what are we gonna do with this. And it's important for your - your long term thing.

Q1: You're smart.

A: So I'm preparing. And so I just asked him, I was like, "Well do you have 401K?" And he was like - he's like, "Yeah I do have that." And then I asked him, I was like, um, I - I didn't ask him like how much that they had or anything but I just said, "Is your lifestyle sustainable?" And he was like, "No."

Q: Okay.

A: And I was like, "How long do you think that's gonna take?" He's like, "I don't know but it's not sustainable."

Q1: Where did his girls go to school?

A: I don't know. He never actually told me, like when I gave - I asked him once, it was like when I was trying to find him an apartment I was like, "Are you comfortable telling me where your girls go to school," that's in the text too, I was like, "So I can figure out what distance from the apartment it is." I was trying to just make his life convenient with like him, his ex, his kids and all the stuff that he needs to do and work. Um, and he was like, "Don't worry about it, their school is pretty centrally located so anywhere in the area that we were discussing will be fine." And he just left it at that. So he didn't even tell me which was fine, I respect that.

Q: Daycare is obviously very expensive for a 2 and - 3 and 5 year old.

A: Oh yeah.

Q: Right. So...

A: I understand.

Q: ...did he ever bring, uh, any - did he ever discuss that?

A: Never.

Q: Okay.

A: Never. Um - uh, like the only - like I said, the only financial thing he ever said is just like, "She just likes to spend money. Like a lot of it."

Q: Okay.

A: So that was just kind of the vibe that I got from that and that it was just - it was a lifestyle that she liked to live, like very like materialistic kind of lifestyle. Like it was...

Q: Wanted to project a certain image...

A: Yes. All the time. And he said that that was why they got that house too, he's like, "She wants everybody to think that we live a certain way and that we can like sustain all this stuff," and he's like, "And we can't." And I told him, I said, "When you're in those situations why don't you," I'm like, "Do you - do you like voice your concern about this?" And he told me, he's like, "When I try to talk to her," he's like, "She's really bossy and she usually shuts me out," and he's like, "When she does that," he's like, "I just let it go." And I was just like, "All right," I mean I don't - I don't try to like interfere with how those two interact. But I didn't ask about it 'cause I'm just curious 'cause I would never put myself in a situation where someone was like, "You know what, we're gonna live in this house that cost like double what we can afford and that's how it's gonna be 'cause I want everybody to think we're fancy." 'Cause I wouldn't do that. I mean to me like I wouldn't put up with somebody doing that to me, and I'm not saying that that's what she was doing. I mean for all I know he could've been completely lying about this, he could be the one spending all the money.

Q: Sure.

A: You know?

Q: This is just what he told you.

A: Exactly. So I mean that's as far as I can interrupt it so I can't be like, "Well oh she needs to do this and she needs to do that," but he - he, you know, he just - he voiced his concern where it's just like, "Financially I'm in a very bad spot that I...

Q: Okay.

A: ...don't need to be in but I'm stuck in," and that was kind of where he was at. So - but I mean he was never like mean when he talked about her, he was never hostile, like nothing like that. He just - I mean very calmly like this is the situation and I think the only reason that he even provided me with that information is because I asked.

Q: Okay. You said something, um, about her being controlling or...

A: Bossy.

Q: …bossy…

A: That's what he said, bossy.

Q: …um, in like a lot of aspects of their life or what - do you know exactly what he meant by that, how that affected him?

A: I think he was just saying when he voices his opinion it's not heard, is - is the gist of that. Which I thought from what it sounded like from their separation from them trying to separate that that was a big deal for him where he was saying that the reason that they don't really get along anymore is because he feels like he's not heard.

Q: Okay.

A: He says that he, you know, he comes home from work and he tries to talk to her and she'll just be like, "One minute, I'm on the phone." Or she'll like scroll through social media and she like doesn't acknowledge him. And, um, he said that he had addressed it with her a few times and their calm, he said they don't really fight, like they don't scream and yell. Um, and he said he had addressed it with her a few times and he said it just fell on deaf ears, he's like, "She just seems like she's not interested anymore," and I think it made him sad because I mean he was like all about his kids and he seemed like he was trying to be all about her but it just wasn't reciprocated and I think at that point he was just like I don't - that it's just they just kind of like fell apart.

Q: Okay.

A: Just kind of drifted apart. But it was…

Q: Was that your wor- was that your words or his?

A: What, that they…

Q: Fell apart.

A: That - I - those are mine.

Q: Okay.

A: Those are mine. He just said that they didn't communicate very well. And it wasn't in a - like a aggressive way communicate, it was just the fact that they didn't like communicate at all.

Q: They just...

A: They didn't talk.

Q: And they had children and they - did - did - do - was there ever mention that he was trying to resolve or, uh, save his marriage to - for the children's sake? Yo- a lot of people talk...

A: Yes.

Q: ...about that, did he talk about that?

A: Yes. I mean he told me that he believed that the only reason that those two had still been doin' it as long as they've been doing - 'cau- he told me that her and him have had communication issues for about six years where she just seems really like detached and uninterested in like trying to like build something with him. Um, and he said - and I said, "Six years is a really long time for you guys to not fix that," considering they were married for what, eight? I mean that's like the majority of their marriage. And he said, um, "Sometimes I think we just do it for the kids," or something like that. I mean it's been a long time since I've seen...

Q: Sure.

A: ...these conversations so I don't know like verbatim but...

Q: And that's - we're trying...

A: ...it was pretty much just like...

Q: ...get you to remember sometimes.

A: Yeah like but he said it wasn't just him though, he was like - I think she does that too...

Q: Okay.

A: ...you know, I mean and it was like this equal part where they are just kind of like goin' through the motions I think.

Q: Mm-hm.

A: And so like when he told me that she was cool with like the 50% everything and just like breakin' it off and being really civil about it it - it kind of made sense to me 'cause I was like the way he made this sound it wasn't oh she's this horrible person or oh I'm this horrible person, it was, "Her and I have drifted so far apart that it's kind of a mutual agreement that this is not gonna work."

Q: So in those six years though they had two children...

A: Yep.

Q: ...um, and you said earlier you did not know she was pregnant until reading the newspaper...

A: Yep.

Q: ...so, um, that never came up in any conversation...

A: Never.

Q: ...um, there was no - no indications that that was going on...

A: None.

Q: ...um, he never hinted to anything like that?

A: Nothing.

Q: As far as you knew, um, he was just leading her, he had two children and, um, that was the final take on that?

A: Yes.

Q: Okay.

A: I think - I know why he lied to me, he lied to me because if I'd have known that he had a child on the way I would have never wasted my time with him in the first place, like none of this would have ever even occurred if he would have just told me the truth.

Q: So do you think if he found out that you, um - if, let's say this week you guys were to go look at some apartments -- and this is hypothetical -- but you, um, you've never found out that his wife was pregnant, would - would that have changed anything? Uh, like you just said, "If I knew he was - his wife was pregnant I wouldn't be in this picture," so if his wife was not pregnant, um, and forgive me but if - if he takes her out of the picture you're never gonna know that she was pregnant, right?

A: What do you mean takes her out of the picture, like...

Q: If - if he murdered her she's out of the picture, you're never gonna know if she was pregnant. If he can get away with murder you're not gonna - I got divorced from my wife...

A1: Wait...

Q: You said - do you understand what I'm saying here? If - if she's gone...

A: But this...

A1: Don't lead.

Q: Hypothetically…

A1: Please. Don't lead on.

Q: Yeah hypothetically if she…

A1: Okay.

Q: …you understand where I'm going? If you didn't know…

A1: Right but you're - you're leading…

Q: Okay.

A1: …into questions that are nothing with your…

Q: If you didn't know though…

A1: Wait Nic.

Q: …that she was there…

A1: Did you hear what I said?

Q: I'm not - I'm following you, I just want her to answer a question that relates to she said something that's important that if he didn't have a child on the way sh- or if he didn't - if she didn't know that she would've continued the relationship, right?

A: But he killed his kids. At what point does he think that I'm gonna be in a relationship?

Q: I'm not t- I'm not talkin' about the children. I'm just talking specifically about her. If i- and if - if you only knew - if the kids were still here and he called you and said, "I'm divorced from my wife," and he gets away with this - do you understand what I'm thinking, from his aspect?

A: I still wouldn't do it. I still wouldn't do it, 'cause I'd be like, "Where did she go?"

Q: Okay.

A: Because I'm under the impression that she's a really good mom. Like, he never bashed her moming skills. Like, he - no. S- no. I wouldn't - no.

Q: Okay.

A: No.

Q: And that's - that - you see where I'm tryin' to take that?

A: Yes.

Q: So he never - you guys never had a conversation about the child, period?

A: I didn't know.

Q: Okay.

A: At all.

Q: All right. And, by your words, if you did know, you would've ended the relationship?

A: Well, because it wouldn't of made sense to me. That he's, like, "I'm getting separated. Oh, by the way, I have a baby on the way." It's, like…

Q: That's 15 weeks.

A: "...You are a liar. You're just tryin' to sleep with me." That's what I would've probably interpreted that as, and I'd a just shut that off at work, and that would've been the end of it.

Q: Okay. Um, all right. We can move past that. Um, the week that he comes back from North Carolina, you - you don't remember, somewhere in the first couple weeks of August?

A: Yeah. I think it was the second week, but I don't remember...

Q: Okay.

A: ...off the top of my head.

Q: So we'll just use August as a timeframe. Is that fair? Because you know...

A: Mm-hm.

Q: ...he left in July, and he comes back in August. How many times do you think you see him?

A: I saw him a few times. I saw him this past Saturday. I saw him the Wednesday before that. And he wanted to see me more. I was the one who wanted my space. I was, like, "Nope. Your kids are home. Go hang out with your kids." And even on Wednesday, I cut it short. Like, he came and hang out with me for a few hours and then I was, like, "Go chill with your kids."

Q: Okay.

A: Um, I was always, like, really respectful of his kids.

Q: Do you know, specifically, where you guys me- went? Did you meet at your hours? Did you guys go to, uh, any restaurants? Did you go to establishments? Where'd you go?

A: Um, last Wednesday he came to my house and this past Saturday, we went to, um - what is the name of that bar that we used to go to? It's not the same - The Lazy Dog, but it's the one off of 144th and I-25. I think it's 144th. Up there.

Q: And it's The Lazy Dog?

A: Yes.

Q: Um, did he ever mention a Rocky's game that night?

A: Um, no. I don't think so. But there was a - there was a, um - the Broncos were playing.

Q: Okay.

A: Which we couldn't see, 'cause they sat us in really crappy spots. But it's okay, 'cause it's pre-season. But, um...

Q: So you we- do you recall what time you went there?

A: Hm, no. I remember - well, kind of. So he had to get a babysitter that night.

Q: Do you know who that was?

A: Uh, somebody who's really young. I remember I asked him who his babysitter was, and he's, like, "We have two. This girl's only 17, but the other one's out of town. So this girl's gonna stay, and she doesn't do overnights. So I gotta be back by 10:00."

Q: Okay.

A: And I remember her sayin' that, and him sayin' that. And I - I don't know what time he got to my house. It was between I want to say, like, 5:30. It might've been 5:00, but I don't think so. 'Cause I think the babysitter, if I remember correctly, showed up at, like, 4:30

or something and he was, like, "I want to spend time getting my kids acclimated to her. And then I will come."

Q: So her chi- his children didn't even know her?

A: Oh, no. They knew her, but he was saying, like, he likes to, like, stay there for a little while. While - he doesn't just, like, walk out the door...

Q: Okay.

A: ...when they show up. It's, like, a transitional thing. And so, um, that's why I'm sayin' I don't know how long that was. I want to say, like, 5:30. And then he had to be back by 10:00, so he left at, like, 9:00-somethin' to be back by 10:00.

((Crosstalk))

Q: So how did he show up? What was he driving?

A: No. He didn't pick me up. He came to my house. We drove my truck.

Q: Okay. So you - he gets to your house. You know what he was driving to get to your house?

A: Um, off the top of my head, I don't remember. Um, h- I'm pretty sure he usually drives that Lexus, but he doesn't always park it in my complex, 'cause the parking - there's not good spaces. So where you guys picked me up at, a lot of times he'll just park out there, because there's room.

Q: Okay.

A: Um, so that kinda works so that he's - 'cause there's just not a lot of room in my apartment complex. Um, but off the top of my head, I don't know what he was driving.

Q: What kinda truck do you drive?

A: I drive a, uh, Toyota 4 Runner.

Q: Okay. So you guys take your 4 Runner to The Lazy Dog?

A: Yep.

Q: And you said they sat you in crappy location? And where…

((Crosstalk))

A: It just…

Q: Where were you put inside the bar?

A: We were - when you walk in, you just hang a right and we were, like, one of the first two booths on the right, when you walk in the door.

Q: Okay.

A: You just - it's just not a good - it's a good spot, but just not for the TVs. And we actually went to the other Lazy Dog. We went to the one that you and me go to. Where's that at? Federal and 100…

A1: 20th.

A: It's 120th and Federal, and we went there, and they have a different menu. And I was, like, "I don't want to eat this food. So we should go to the other one."

Q: So initially you go to the 120th location?

A: Yes.

Q: Did you actually…

A: And...

Q: ...get seated?

A: Uh, kinda, sorta. They were, like, cleaning off a table and we were standing there, just kinda lookin' at the beer menu and the food menu, and I was, like, "I don't want this." And he - and so we left.

Q: Six o'clock?

A: Probably somewhere around there. 6:00, 6:30. And then we left and went to the other one, and we ate dinner.

Q: All right. And you were in the first or second booth, right...

A: Ah-huh.

Q: ...to the right of the door?

A: Ah-huh.

Q: I'm just askin', 'cause if they have video, we want to be able to verify that.

A: Ah-huh.

Q: So that's why it's important.

A: Ah-huh.

Q: Um, and you were there for how long?

A: Uh, I don't know. Probably - we didn't stay for dessert, so I don't know. How long's the restaurant take? Like, an hour-and-a-half?

((Crosstalk))

Q1: I don't know.

Q: I've never been to The Lazy Dog.

A: I don't know. Probably about an hour-and-a-half, and then, uh, we went back to my house for a little bit. Hung out at my house, um, for a little while, and then he had to leave. And then he left.

Q: Do you recall what time he left?

A: Off the top of my head, no. I remember he was, like, gonna be late to be back at 10:00. I think there's a text message where he starts texting me when he's home at his house.

Q: Okay.

A: So you can probably figure that out. And I remember th- I texted him back and I was, like, "Damn, that was quick." Or "Wow, that was really quick." He's, like, "Yeah, I even had time to stop at the ATM," or "Stop at the gas station." Stop somewhere to get money to pay the babysitter.

Q: Okay.

A: Um, and I was just, like, thinkin', like, "Whoa, that was really fast." Um, but I think he was still, like, a little late coming back, but nothing too drastic. So he probably left my house, like, somewhere around 9:30-ish.

Q: All right. And you n- he goes straight home. He texts you. Um...

A: Well, I was already home.

Q: Right. No, he text you. He goes straight home from your house and he texts you that he's home?

A: Mm-hm.

Q: So that should be in your text messages.

A: Uh - uh, it should be. I'm pretty positive that was not a phone call. I'm almost positive that was a text. Sometimes I get them flip-flopped, or I don't remember, but sometimes I know. I'm pretty sure that one was a text.

Q: Saturday, during your dinner, um, what - what kinda conversation did you guys have?

A: Uh, I don't even remember. Oh. I, uh - so he's been tryin' to, like, eat a little healthier than he normally does. And he's always, like, been in the workin' out since I knew him and he, like, tries to eat clean. But he was tryin' to, like, step it up a little bit. And nothing like the people who do, like, the competitions and the shows that are all super restrictive. I mean, it was nothin' like that. It's just, like, day-to-day general maintenance, but it's how I eat and it's pretty healthy. And, um, he's been losin' a lot of weight. He lost I want to say, like, 13 pounds in the time that we were hangin' out. And, honestly, when you start eatin' a little bit cleaner and you start workin' out a little bit harder, the first couple months - especially for a man, 'cause they lose weight faster - it's not something that's, like, that drastic, to me, but it did stand out that it was, like, a little much. And so I was, like, "Whoa. Like, maybe you're not eating enough macro nutrients. So let me look at them." So he had been working on his My Fitness Pal app and, like, programming, like, all the stuff he eats. And I just started going through them and I was, like, tryin' to figure out, like, where his ratios were wrong. We actually spent a lot of time doing that, 'cause he had asked me to do it for him. Um, because I just was at the point where I was, like, if his weight loss slows down in a few weeks, he'll be fine. And if it doesn't, then his macros are a little off. It's not, like, that big of a deal, like, in the workout community. This is, like, a very normal thing, but I just...

Q: Did you have any other outside concerns? Like, potential drug use? Alcohol use? Any of that stuff that - that led you do go, "Hey, he's lost an extreme amount of weight in such a short period of time"?

A: No, and I wouldn't call it extreme. It was just, like - it w- it was - it was a lot but, I mean, I - when I first started workin' out, I dropped, like, 12 pounds in two weeks. When I first, first started, like, hittin' it hard with the diet. So the fact that he lost, like, that much weight, it wasn't - like I said, it was - it was not a surprising amount. I just didn't want it to be, like, a sustained amount. But no, I didn't think anything weird of it just because of, like, how interknitted I am with the, like, workout community and I know, like, this is possible. But it just - he - the thing that concerned me about it, I guess - and it wasn't even concern, but the thing that, like, kinda red-lighted me, like, "Hey, this might be con- carrying on," is the fact that his macros were, like, pretty dialed in. Like, I had wrote them and he, like, didn't stay exactly on them, but his calorie intake was about where it needed to be. My experience, anyways, for, like, what he was trying to achieve. And so I don't know. He didn't seem to have a problem with it. He liked where he was at with all of that.

Q: So that was your main conversation Saturday?

A: That was, like, a big chunk while we were there. Is, like, us actually going through - 'cause I was, like, going through each item. Like, "Why do you have - why are your ratios off?"

((Crosstalk))

Q: Do you know where his kids or wife were that night?

A: On Saturday?

Q: Yeah. His ki- well, you know his kids are with the babysitter. Do you know where his wife is?

A: She's in Arizona.

Q: Okay. How do you know that?

A: 'Cause he told me.

Q: Okay.

((Crosstalk))

Q: Do you know what she's doing there?

A: I think she's on a business trip. He didn't even tell me right away. He actually told me, I think, like, on Saturday or somethin'.

((Crosstalk))

Q: Like, during…

((Crosstalk))

A: Friday or somethin'. I don't - I honestly don't remember. I just remember I was, like, really surprised. Where he's, like, "Hey, like, I'm gonna try to get a babysitter if you want to hang out or somethin' like that." And I was, like, "Why do you need a babysitter? Like, your wife's home." He's, like, "No, she's out of town." I was, like, "Oh."

Q: Okay.

A: "Okay."

Q: Was there much conversation regarding that? Her on - bein' on a trip, or the children on - during those conversations?

A: Not really. I just asked him what time she was comin' home on Sunday and he just said, "Really late."

Q: Okay.

A: And that was it. I mean, i- i- there's nothin' really to talk about with that.

Q: Okay. So your conversations mainly health-related?

A: Mm-hm.

Q: Um, you guys returned to your house and then he goes home. And then you talked to him for, um, a few hours on Sunday.

A: Did I? Are you asking me or are you telling me?

Q: I'm asking you.

A: Oh. I was, like, I don't even know. Sunday - honestly - oh, on s- so wait a minute. That was Saturday. This is the - we're talking about Saturday. We're not talking about Sunday right now.

Q: Okay. So you're still on Saturday?

A: Yes. This...

Q: You guys have a phone conversation when he gets home?

A: That was the day that he got the babysitter and I went out to dinner. Not on Sunday.

Q: Okay.

A: Okay. Sorry, I just want to make sure you got...

Q: That's okay. Yep.

A: ...your days right. So Saturday, yes. We went out. He had the babysitter. He went home. I'm sure we did. We always talk on the phone and, honestly, I mean, (Mark) asked me that the other day. He's, like, "How long were you on the phone? 15 minutes? 20 minutes?" Like, you're gonna have to look at the records, to be honest with you. Like, I'm - so much.

Q: You like to talk. I can tell a little bit.

A: Yeah.

((Crosstalk))

A: A little bit.

A1: 400 - when she was young, she'd crank out about 400 words a minute. Gusts, up to 600. That little thing can yack, man.

Q: You're a talker. So I'm - I'm lettin' you talk. Um...

A1: I need to use a restroom. If I can use...

Q: Let me show you where it's at.

A: Can you get me some water...

Q: So...

A: ...while you're out there with them, please?

A1: Sure.

A: Thank you.

A1: And another bottle?

Q: That's...

A: Yeah. At least one.

Q: Let's move to...

A: Sunday.

Q: ...Sunday, right? Well, let me reverse somethin'. Your conversation with the children - or about the children, was there ever any talk about medical concerns with either of the children?

A: All I know is (CiCi) is allergic to pea- not peanuts. Like, pine nuts. Pine nuts.

Q: So she has a nut allergy?

A: Yes.

Q: Did they take meds?

A: He - I know that she had, like, an epi-pen, but as far as I know, she didn't have any meds. But I never asked. Like, I was just told, like, she has a pretty severe allergy. And...

Q: Enough to carry an epi-pen. That's pretty severe.

A: Yeah. While we're on this, so when he was in North Carolina, um - this is all, like, hearsay now, because it's, like, this is in a conversation. Like, he's telling me this stuff, but who knows exactly what happened? But he went out there to go see his family and her family, and while he was in town, before he went out to North Carolina, I guess his mother had accidentally, like - not exposed her to something with nuts, but had, like, given a product - I think it was, like, ice cream, to a different kid that could have traces of nuts. Or something - I don't know. But it was, like, his daughter was fine, but she was, like, in the range of contamination and I think his wife was very upset about that. And when he got to North Carolina, he told me that he was supposed to spend, like, half time with them, half the time with her family, and that was supposed to be what it was. I don't know. But he said that he went to go see his family, and they weren't answering the phone for, like, a day or two before he went out there. And then, when he got there, there was a note on the door that said, uh, "Son, if you stop by, we're at the beach." And they ignored him for, like, most of the time that he was out there. And...

Q: His own family?

A: Yes. His mom, his dad, and his sister.

Q: What'd he - what's the significance? Do you know under - do you know why?

A: Yeah. He said - and, again, I don't know what is true...

Q: Mm-hm.

A: ...with this man anymore, and what's not. But he told me that - like, leading up to it, I was, like, "Well, why are your folks, like, ignoring you?" And I was, like, really concerned about this. Like, every single day he would talk to me when he was out there and I was, like, "You talk to your family today? You talk to your family today? Did you talk to your dad? What happened? Did you talk to them?" "No, I didn't." Or, "Yeah, I talked to my mom." "Well, what'd she say? Are you gonna hang out with them?" Like, I wanted him to see his people, because it's important. Family is an important thing, you know? It just needs to function properly and...

Q: Sure.

A: ...and so I was, like, "Well, um" - and he was, like, "Well, they're ignoring me." And I was, like, "What do you think happened?" And he was, like, "I'm not really sure, but I think, um, something was said between my wife and them during that incident." And he's, like...

Q: The...

A: "...because every time I..."

Q: ...peanut or...

A: Yes.

Q: ...fruit and nut...

A: That happened before he got there. Yes. And he was, like, "Because every time that I try to, um - I talk about possibly going over there to see if they're home, she gets upset about it." And I was, like, "Okay." And he told me that his mom and his wife did not get along at all. He said that his mom didn't even show up to his wedding, because she's, like, really - did not care for Shanann. So again, I don't know what's true and what's not, but I just know that there was, like, some tension there.

Q: Mm-hm.

A: And, again, like, that part is, like - I feel like it's almost third-party, so that's why it's, like...

Q: Sure.

A: ...I didn't even worry about...

((Crosstalk))

Q: Well, but it came from him to you, so it's not. It is somethin' that I, um - is - whether it's important or not, we can validate that. Uh, I'm sure we will be having some conversations with family. Um, you know, it - what does it mean? I don't know. Um, but...

A: Yeah. I don't know, either. But I just know...

Q: So...

A: ...like...

Q: Maybe she n- I don't know.

A: Well, and then, um, he ended up seeing them on the last, like, full day that he was there, and they told him, supposedly, that she had gotten really upset and then scream and yelled in front of his s- Chris's sisters kids that are very young. And that his mom and his dad had said, like, "You're never gonna see Chris again. You're gonna see me. You're never gonna see the babies." And just, like, threatened them. And then, like, walked off. And I guess that was the incident that happened prior to him coming out there. And then she didn't tell him about it.

Q: Mm-hm.

A: She just, like, let it go and then he just spent all week tryin' to figure out why his family was, like...

Q: Hm.

A: ...not tryin' to be involved.

Q: Gotcha.

A: Um, so again, I'm not sure. That was i- like, it - it just feels really third-party, so it's hard for me to, like, talk about. Because...

Q: Sure.

A: ...I don't know how much...

Q: That's okay.

A: ...validation...

((Crosstalk))

Q: So be- beyond the me- the nut allergy for (CiCi), did you know of any other - did she take meds that you know of? Other than carrying an epi-pen?

A: His kids or his wife?

Q: No, hi- his children.

A: No.

Q: And now - well, if you know anything about his wife's medical conditions, if she had any.

A: No. I've, like, read in the newspaper. They keep sayin', "Oh, she had medical conditions." And I'm like, "Is that a misprint? Are they talkin' about (CiCi)? Or is that just somethin' else I don't know?"

Q: So you don't know anything about...

A: Nope.

Q: ...uh, Shanann having any kind of medical problems?

A: Nope.

Q: Okay. Covered Saturday. So there's a phone call Saturday night, actually. Um, from - uh, it can't be Saturday. It had to be Sunday. I wrote that down quickly. Sunday night. Is there anything else you think - let's - let me just back up. From the Saturday, where you guys had a meal at - at The Lazy Dog, to prior for the six weeks that you guys were serious - and, um, although your dad's here and I think you're probably pretty comfortable, your relationship with Chris was - can you describe your relationship?

A: I mean, when he was with me, I considered it to be fairly healthy. Was open communication and it was what I thought was honest. And it was very calm. It was respectful. Uh, we got along really well. He gave me my space when I needed it. I gave him his. And any time, like, he wanted to take care of hi like, any time that his kids could be in, like, his life for hours or days or whatever - whenever they were home, I made sure that I wasn't a presence in his life. So that he could be the best dad that he needed to be. Um, and, I mean, I thought what we had - it was very comfortable for me. I enjoyed it. I think he did very much, as well.

Q: Your guys - you - six to eight weeks, two mo- whatever it was, you guys have an intimate relationship during that time?

A: Yes.

Q: Okay. So you're - and you're pretty serious. Um, d- did he ever tell you that he loved you?

A: Yes, he did.

Q: Did you ever tell him the same?

A: Couple times.

Q: Okay. Um, notwithstanding that today, 'cause that may - those thoughts may have changed for you, but on - let's go Mon- Sunday into Monday or Monday, did you - did you still love him on those days?

A: I think it was something where it was, like, I s- I said it a few times and I meant it, but he definitely felt the urge to say it to me a lot more than I did to him. Because it was just all very new to me and it was, like, "Take your time with this. Like, you don't need to - to, like, rush that, you know?" Like, I remember when he was in North Carolina and he was, like, tryin' to patch things up with his wife. And he told me he loved me. And I was, like, "Don't say that to me. Like, please go try to fi- and I mean it." And that might be in the texts, too. Where it's, like, "Don't. Don't. Like, don't say those words to me and then go try to make peace with you li- wife and lay in bed with another woman. Like, just don't do that." And I was, like, "It's not that I don't appreciate what you're saying to me." It's, like, just - it just didn't sit right for me, you know? So I'd just be like…

Q: Almost like an insecurity where he had to say that to you? Or…

A: I - I don't - no. I think he - he, like - looking back at all this now, I don't think he was trying to fix things with her. So saying "I love you" to me seemed like probably something that he genuinely meant. Like, "I love this woman." And regardless of where he was gonna end up that night. But, to me, in the way that I was perceiving things, he had told me that he was tryin' to fix things with her. So it's just, like, "This is an inappropriate time." And I wasn't mad at him. And I'm pretty sure that's in the texts, too. Where it was very, like, calm but it's just, like, it's almost disrespectful. Where it's, like, "Please don't." I'm like, "You know, if we get to that point where it is you and me, like, yes, you can say that. But don't - not then. Like, that's..."

Q: So you thought he was very genuine when he said that?

A: I - yeah. I did. I mean, and he wrote it and sent all those cards I gave you. Not in all of them, but, like...

Q: Hm.

A: ...the later ones.

Q: And...

A: Thank you.

Q: When you said it to him, you said you meant it, when you said it.

A: Yes. I just didn't say it as frequently as he said it. Like, sometimes he would say it and I was just, like - for me, it was still, like, very, very new. So I kinda, like, took my time and only said it when I was just, like, "This is a really important moment."

Q: So you go- I mean, in the short period of time that you guys were together, he...

A: Yes.

Q: ...wa- became very attached to you.

A: Yes. Very, very attached.

Q: I mean, he's sending cards...

A: Flowers.

Q: ...he's tellin' you he loves you, he sends you flowers. Does he buy you any other gifts?

A: Nope. I wouldn't have wanted them anyways. It's - flowers is enough. You can't - I don't need expensive stuff.

Q: Okay. But he becomes very attached to you.

A: Yes.

Q: Um, you guys are talking multiple times a day, at least. You're...

((Crosstalk))

A: All the time.

Q: You're seein' each other on a regular basis.

A: Yep.

Q: Um, so i- it - it's a very, um - and - and his wife is not around, nor are his children. So there's a lot of time for you guys to build your relationship in this first four - four weeks or so. Is that fair?

A: Yeah. And even when she - she was back, I mean, it was still, like, we were still spending time together. He was still spending time with his children, and I have my own life. Like, I mean, there was one week where I just, like, went out of town for my - with my friends for my birthday. I wasn't even around the whole, like, th- last few days of June, up until the 3rd of July. I was, like, gone. You know? And then there was another - like, a f- last weekend, I had a friend impromptu come in town from out of state, and I hosted her, uh, for a few days. And it's, like, it - like, I still did my own thing all the time. Like, whether he was there or not. Like, if my friends were, like, "Hey, we want to make plans," I would tell him, like, "We're not hangin' out today, 'cause I want to go see my mom or my dad."

Q: Did your friends know about him?

A: Nope.

Q: Why?

A: 'Cause it's - like, he's with two women right now. They don't...

Q: Okay.

A: ...need to know about that.

Q: So if you had a boyfriend of four to eight weeks, on a regu- I don't know if you ha- were married prior or if you had a boyfriend before, but if you had a steady boyfriend, you would let people know - I think you told me before we got started that y- you just told your dad about Chris, um...

A: No, I wouldn't of told him.

Q: ...recently.

A: I wouldn't of told people.

Q: Okay.

A: It's too early. I mean, people...

Q: So you don't tell your friends, "Hey, I have a new boyfriend"?

A: No, 'cause they - i- people come and go.

Q: Okay.

A: I mean, dating, seeing these days is, like - it sucks. I mean, so no. I wouldn't. I mean, it would have to be somethin' - even with (Shawn). I think I was with (Shawn) for probably, like, six or seven months before I brought him home to my family. I mean, I really - and same with...

Q: Okay.

A: ...the - that was the guy I was in a previous relationship with. But I mean...

Q: But this one, you were a little bit more - you said he's with two women. Did that - was that one of your considerations for not telling anybody about him?

A: Y- yes. Well, I mean, it was, like, "Okay. Like, this" - to me, it wasn't gonna be an ex- extended thing. Like, if it got to the point where we were, like, dating for, like, three or four months and he's still talkin' about, "Oh, I'm gonna move out and I'm gonna sell the house," I think at that point I probably would've just been like, "I don't think you're really, like, doing these things you say you're gonna do." And I probably would've just, like, left. Because, at that point, it's not fair. It wasn't fair to me in the first place. It wasn't fair to her in the first place. It wasn't fair to any of us in the first place. You know? It wasn't fair to his family, for him to have an affair. It wasn't fair to me to have him lie to me and make me think that everything is going to plan and, still, to this day, I don't even know what's a lie and what's not. I don't even know if they were, like, filing for divorce. I don't know if they were putting the house up. I don't even know - I don't even know anymore what is real and what is not.

Q: Sure.

A: But what I do know is it's just, like - you know, that wasn't fair to me, either, because if I'd a known not even all the truth but, like, obviously, some of it, I wouldn't have even engaged in any of this in the first place. And it just - and I mean, and that's the part, for me, just, like, on my personal level, outside of everything that is happening. That is gonna affect me long-term. It's, like, you know, I'm gonna wake up every day and know that, like, this mom and her unborn child and these two little girls are not around anymore. And it breaks my heart. It is so - oh my god. And - and he - and then I have to think about, like, the consequences of his actions, and how they affect everybody else. Like, all of these - her family's impacted. My name is about to be, like, slandered for probably a while. I don't know how long it's gonna take to heal, but I would not be surprised if it's gonna be hard to go out in public sometimes for a couple of years. And that really hurts me. I'm just, like, this is a horrible, horrible thing. Like, how dare you? You know? And - and people aren't gonna understand that. You know? They're gonna say, "Oh, you know, you're the woman that had an affair with this man who took out his whole family." And I take a step back and it's just, like, I didn't know. Like, I - I - uh. It's - he's so disgusting. I am so ashamed of him and everything, and I just - oh, those little girls. They're so little. They're so little.

Q: We talked to - we talked a little bit earlier about gettin' some help for these things, and we can provide that.

A: God.

A1: Okay.

Q: At - at really, no cost. Through the state.

A1: Oh, one more can - we just want to make sure, uh, there's resolution.

Q: Absolutely.

A1: That's why we come to you guys.

Q: Yeah.

A1: To pound this sh…

Q: And…

A1: …pound it down until there's…

Q: Yeah, I - I'm…

A1: …nothin' left.

Q: …sorry that you're talking again today. I really am. I don't want to put you through any more trauma than you've already been through. There is, um, reasons for everything that we're doing today and what - what occurred. And I'm sorry. I genuinely am sorry. I - it - these are not things that we like to do twice. It's the same thing with other types of victims from other crimes. We want to do it once, and we want to be done. Unfortunately, we didn't know yesterday, uh, what we know today. And that's why we're here, because we need this video. And I'm - I am sorry, 'cause I know it's hard to talk about it. But it - it's…

((Crosstalk))

A: …so sad, and she's pregnant.

A1: And - and wo- on our end, we didn't…

A: God, they're so cute. They're so little. Like, wow. Why? Why? Why? Why? How? I don't even understand how you could, like, bring yourself to do that to somebody who's, like, that big. Oh, Jesus.

Q: Take a minute. Do you want to step out for a minute?

A: No, I just need to chill with my eyes closed for a sec. I still cannot believe this is happening. All right. Let's keep goin', 'cause we're just…

((Crosstalk))

A: ...gettin' to, like, the meat of this whole...

Q: Let's - let's...

A: ...situation.

Q: ...get to the phone call on Saturday, from 9:00 to 11:00.

A: Uh...

Q: What did you guys - or s- pardon me. On Sunday from 9:00 to 11:00.

A: Yeah. We talked a few times. So Sunday...

A1: You okay?

A: I think so. I need to think. I can't even think.

Q: Take a couple breaths and take a - take a second.

A: Sunday night. I don't even know. I don't think I was that concerned about anything at that point.

Q: You guys had had a meal - a nice meal the night before. You knew his wife was probably coming home late that evening.

A: Oh. Um, you know what? I still don't remember what we talked about. I, like - honestly, like, we talked about so much random stuff. Like, it's so hard to pinpoint some of these things. Um, I don't remember what we talked about. I do remember that was a long phone conversation, though. We probably talked about all sorts of stuff. Um, one thing...

Q: Anything...

A: ...I do remember, though, um, that I didn't remember earlier when I was talking to (Mark) - so this is, like, where I'm starting to remember, like, little bits and pieces.

Q: Mm-hm.

A: I - I don't remember...

((Crosstalk))

A: Yeah. No. This was a phone conversation. I don't remember what was in the phone conversation. Probably nothing of relevance, to be honest with you. But, um, usually he talks to me when he's, like, down in the basement, in his bed, before he goes to bed and before I go to bed. And I could hear the TV on, which I thought was kinda weird. I didn't ask him, I just heard it in the background, and I remember thinking - and it was, like, right before we got off the phone. I was, like, "Why the hell is he up?" And there's, like, no TV downstairs. So I was, like, "Well, maybe" - I don't know.

Q: So no TV in the basement, where he usually calls you from?

A: Yeah. And I don't know how many TVs they have. Like, I've never been in their bedroom. Like, I went upstairs once and it was, like, to their little play room and I just, like, looked at it. And I was, like, "That's super cute that your girls have books." And that was, like, it. And other than that, I have never been in any of those rooms in that upstairs. Like, to me, it was just, like, you don't - no. Like, ever. I had no - so I don't know if he has any other TVs. I'm assuming by, like, how much other nice stuff they have in their house, it wouldn't surprise me. So I'm not quite sure what room he was in at that point. Um, but I just remember hearing the TV, and I was, like - it was just weird to me, 'cause I was, like, "Why are you watching TV right now? It is, like, super late." And that was the only thing...

Q: And he - and he had phoned you or were you guys already talking when the TV was goin' or just...

A: I just remember, like, I - like, go- picked up on it, like, later, but I don't think it was, like, throughout the whole conversation.

Q: Okay.

A: Like, I just remember it being towards the end, 'cause I remember thinking, like, "Wow, it's really late."

Q: The - the, um - somethin' I didn't ask you about the house, 'cause you'd been there twice and it just, uh, made me remember. Do you remember how you guys accessed the house?

A: Uh, that's a good question. Uh, so once through the garage, and I think once through the front door.

Q: Uh...

A: I think the first time was through the front door. I think. And I think the second time was through the garage.

Q: Is there anything unique about either of the doors when you went into the house? That might not be typical of another house?

A: Like, a unique door? I know they have a...

Q: Not the door itself.

A: ...camera on their door.

Q: Okay. There's - there's...

A: I mean, I know that.

Q: There's a camera on the - which door?

A: I - it's on the front door, isn't it?

Q: Um, I don't know. I'm asking you.

A: I think so.

Q: Okay.

A: Uh, I don't know. Um…

Q: Was - did he use a key to access the house?

A: No. Um, he did not. The first time I went over there, he just let me in. And then the second time - did we go through the garage? I don't remember. I've been through his garage before. I went through his front door once, though. 'Cause I remember he had just cleaned - it was the first time I went through his front door. 'Cause he had just cleaned his carpets, and he had moved all the furniture out of the way, and the furniture was kind of in the way of the door. And he's, like, "The door doesn't open all the way right now. I'll move all the furniture back when the carpet dries." So I do remember that, just kinda offhandedly. Uh, and the second time, I want to say we went through his garage, 'cause I remember his garage. I remember - yeah. Yeah. So…

Q: So he was at the house when you went there? Um, you were never there by yourself, correct?

A: He was at - yeah, no.

Q: Or he took you there?

A: He - the first time, he was already there…

Q: Okay.

A: …and I met up with him. And the second time, we went there together.

Q: So the front door - I asked if he had used a key.

A: He let me in.

Q: Okay. So there's a, um - you know, those key pads...

A: Mm-hm.

Q: ...where you can enter a access code. Do you remember seein' that on his door?

A: Oh, like, I want to say vaguely, but to be honest with you, I don't remember. Like, he let me in that day. That's - that was so long...

Q: So he never gave you...

A: ...ago.

Q: He never gave you the code to access his home?

A: No.

Q: Okay.

A: Not at all.

Q: Um, you talk about a security system. Uh, there was a s- uh, camera on the front door?

A: Mm-hm.

Q: Was that just, like, a - you know what a ring doorbell is? That goes to your phone?

A: I don't even know what it looked like.

Q: Okay.

A: I only know that it existed, either because A, I wasn't paying attention the first time I was over there but, B, because of all the stuff that's going on right now. That's the only...

Q: Okay.

A: ...reason I know it's...

Q: Okay.

A: ...e- it exists.

Q: Do you remember seeing any cameras anywhere in the house?

A: No.

Q: Okay. Did he ever tell you about the alarm system or give you an access code...

A: No.

Q: ...to the alarm system?

A: No, no, no. I wouldn't have asked for that. I wouldn't of wanted that anyways.

Q: Sorry to regress to that.

A: No, you're okay.

Q: We can go back to the - the phone call. Or where you noticed the television in the background...

A: Yeah.

Q: ...of the phone call.

A: Yep. So I didn't know what room he was in, but I was just, like - I just thought it was weird. 'Cause he's always, like - before I go to bed and I lay down, he's always, like, kinda tryin' to do the same thing. We just talk. It's, like, a really chill thing 'til one of us is about to pass out. Then that's, like, the end of it. Um, but it was strange. 'Cause I was, like, "The TV's on." And I remember what I was thinkin'. I was, like, "Maybe he's waitin' up for her." And then I was, like, "Maybe not." I didn't know. I didn't - it wasn't something that, like, alerted me. It was just different from his...

((Crosstalk))

A: ...standard operating procedure. Because he - whether his wife is home or she's gone, he's always got kinda, like, the standard op when he calls me. So that's why it was kind of, like, unique.

Q: Okay.

A: Because it doesn't really fluctuate when she's there and when she's not there. He's pretty, like, free rein with what he does.

Q: Mm-hm. So anything i- anything important that you recall during that conversation about the children, about his wife, about what he was doing the next day, what he had planned? Anything like that?

A: No.

Q: Did he tell you any of that information?

A: I remember he told he had to go to the field and not to the office on Monday morning.

Q: Okay. Did he specifically say where he needed to go on Monday morning?

A: No. I don't ask him for those sites. There's li- Anadarko's got, like, thousands of sites. If he were to tell me, I wouldn't of - I wouldn't even tell...

Q: They're just, like, random numbers and stuff, right?

A: Well, he told me - he said, "I gotta go to a site. I gotta go, um, check out, like, a valve" or somethin' where they think that they had a release. Somethin' like that. Uh...

Q: Did he mention the town or anywhere...

A: No. No. He just told me that that's what he had to go do.

Q: Okay.

A: He's, like - 'cause, yeah. He was, like, "I won't see you in the office in the morning." 'Cause I usually - I see him, but I don't actually, like, talk to him. Like, I'll go in the cafeteria. I will put my lunch in the fridge, and him and his whole team are sitting in there, and I don't talk to any of them. I just walk out. Um, but anyways, yeah. He's, like, "So I won't see you. I'm goin' to the field." Which is not an uncommon thing for the Ops guys to, like, just go straight to the field. Like, it happens. Like, typically, they go to the office. I would say, like, three or four days a week. But there are days where him and his other team members are not there. Or, like, I'll get in there and some days the - the cafeteria's packed, and they're all there. And other days, I get in there, and there's only, like, three or four of them.

Q: So it didn't cause you any concern that he said...

A: No.

Q: "...I'm goin' to the field on Monday. I won't see you"? That wasn't...

A: No. It didn't...

Q: That's happened before?

A: Yeah, I mean…

Q: Okay.

A: …it wasn't something - I mean, and it's not just him. It's, like, that whole team. Like, you can just tell when they've got, like, a lot goin' on. 'Cause I'll walk in and there'll be, like, two of them as opposed to, like, six or seven.

Q: Do you know what he did Sunday, during the day?

A: Um, I don't even know what I did on Sunday during the day. I am so tired. Let me just think about this. (Daniel) came over Friday. I hung out with him Saturday. And then Sunday…

Q1: When did (Jim) come in?

A: Monday.

Q1: Huh.

A: (Jim) got here Monday. What did I do on Sunday? I am, like, drawing a blank. I'm really tired. I don't know. Can I get back to you on that?

Q: Did you guys have any conversations on Saturday night during your meal, what he might be doing on Sunday?

A: I'm sure we did. I don't know why I'm drawing a blank, 'cause I haven't slept.

Q: I- if I say that his - he may have, uh, done something with his children, would that refresh…

A: Oh, yes.

Q: ...your memory?

A: He went to a birthday party.

Q: Okay. Um, do you know whose house he was going to?

A: Nope, but I know that they had a water balloon fight.

Q: Okay. He - he had one or his children?

A: His children did.

Q: Okay.

A: He said he used to get really into it. He said he got, like, really interactive with his kids. He's, like, "So many adults don't really spend a lot of time playing with the kids, but I always do."

A1: We went to the museum on what day? Saturday or Sunday?

A: Sunday.

A1: Okay.

A: That's right.

A1: Okay.

A: So - yeah, that's what I was, like, "Was I hanging out with you?" God. Uh, so...

Q: Very memorable event, huh?

A: Uh, we hi...

A1: That was, uh...

A: Me and him and my - my m- stepmother...

A1: My wife and...

A: ...and my sister went...

A1: Yeah.

A: ...to, uh, the museum. And that's right.

Q: What museum?

A: Uh, the Denver Museum of Nature and Science. And they went to brunch prior to that, and I skipped brunch. Um, and I went to the gym.

A1: You shouldn't of. It was good.

A: I had to do core day. That was the last time I worked, actually. Um...

A1: That's what we did Sunday. Okay.

A: And - yeah. So core day, and then we went - we went to the museum, and then, um...

Q: When did you - did he tell you about the water balloon fight on Sunday evening, during your conversation on the phone?

A: I think so.

Q: Okay. So...

A: I think so.

Q: ...you don't know whose house he went to on Sunday?

A: No.

Q: Um, but you knew it was for a child's birthday?

A: Yeah. And he had told me about that in advance, really. So I don't know if it was Saturday that he had told me that he was gonna go to the birthday or, like, Friday. I just remember he was, like, "I gotta go to this birthday party…"

Q: Okay.

A: "…with my kids."

Q: Um, any other conversation that makes sense?

A: I mean, honestly, at this point, I'm really tired, so I know there are certain things that I need to tell you guys that we'll get to as these days progress.

Q: Yep.

A: Um, but in all honesty, if it doesn't stand out to me now…

Q: Today?

A: …it probably wasn't…

Q: That's fine.

A: …relevant.

A1: What about that 9 o'clock thing you were tellin' me on Monday?

A: Oh, what he told me? Oh, yeah. Well, we'll get there. We'll get there. We're still on Sunday night.

Q: So we're on Sunday.

A: We're - we're gonna go…

((Crosstalk))

Q: We're gonna get - we're gonna get to...

A: This is gonna be a long day.

Q: We're gonna get there to Monday. We're - we're getting there. So Sunday night - or Sunday during the day, you had your own personal, um, stuff going on...

A: Mm-hm.

Q: ...with your family.

A: Mm-hm.

Q: You never see him on Sunday. Is that accurate?

A: No. I didn't see him. What did I do the rest of the day? I came home. I think I might've just chilled at my house. I don't remember. I think I cleaned my house. I don't know. I didn't see him, though.

Q: Okay. And...

A: Yeah. Saturday was the last time I saw him.

Q: Okay. Sunday, you're at home. You talk to him from - we know he - you have a conversation...

A: Mm-hm.

Q: ...in the late evening hours, and then...

A: Mm-hm.

Q: ...you go to sleep?

A: Mm-hm.

Q: Um, on Sunday night?

A: Mm-hm.

Q: When's the next time you talk with Chris?

A: Probably Monday morning.

Q: Do you know what - what time?

A: No. I mean, so we used to, like, randomly text each other, like, throughout the day. But we both get really busy. So some days, like, I don't hear a lot from him, and some days I don't text him until, like, 2 o'clock in the afternoon. 'Cause I'm just, like, busy. And I - I remember, I didn't hear a lot from him that day. Uh, which was, like - that's not out of the normal for either one of us, um, during the day. Um, but at one point, I do remember he, like, text me and he's, like, "Oh, it's been a really busy day." And then, like, said some other stuff. Which I'm sure you will find in my text. What he said, I don't know. It wasn't obviously, anything that was, like, alerting to me. L- that's what I'm sayin'. Like, at this point, like, I remember really key things. But if it's, like, a conversation, then I'm like, "I don't remember exactly what was discussed." It's 'cause it was probably just bullshit. Like, just...

Q: Just...

A: ...talkin' to each other. Yeah.

Q: ...small talk stuff?

A: Yeah. Um, but I remember he was busy that day, and we didn't talk that much. And then I - I clocked out at 3:00 is what my timecard says. That's what I was showing, um, (Mark), the other day. And I got home to go meet my buddy. One of my good friends was comin' over to my house. And he actually has a key to my house. So he was actually there when I got there. And...

Q: Who's that?

A: My friend, (Jim). Um, and so (Jim) came over and I got home. He was there. He had, like, just walked in the door, and, um, I remember, like, briefly, after he got there, I checked my texts. I mean, briefly after I met up with (Jim), I, like, glanced at my texts and Chris said something about, like, "My family's not home." Or, like, "My wife and kids aren't home." Like, something to that effect. And I told (Mark) - 'cause he asked me for a time, and I don't have an exact time, but 'I remember it was, like, right after I walked in the...

Q: That was a text message, though?

A: Yeah. It's in a text. And it's, like - it was, like, briefly after I walked in the door. So based off how long it takes me to get home from work and when I clocked out, it was probably about 3:45 PM. Um, text me and tells me that. And, like, he knows when I get off of work, too. So he doesn't always bug me if I'm busy. So I don't know what's up with that, but that's when he - that's when he sends that to me. And, um...

Q: So you're saying that he - he would've known that you would've had your phone available to you and not been at work when he sent you that text message?

A: Uh, yes. That's what I'm trying to say.

Q: So looking back at it, you think it was purposefully sent at that time?

A: Oh, I'm sure.

Q: Is - I'm - the - I'm just asking your feeling on that.

A: Yes. And then he said, "Call me when you can." And I was, like...

Q: There was no other communication between you and him that morning, on Monday morning, at all?

A: Well, there w- there was, but it was, like, random, like...

Q: It - but nothin' about this event?

A: No. No, no, no, no, no.

Q: About, like, "My mo- my wife's missing" or...

A: No.

Q: "...My" - w- anything?

A: Nothin'.

Q: Okay.

A: Nothin'.

Q: And you knew he wasn't comin' to the office, 'cause he had told you that Sunday night.

A: Yeah. And then he goes - and so like, they're only in the office for the morning. Like...

Q: Right.

A: ...some days it's longer than others, but I would say by a maximum of 7:30, every single morning, they are all gone. And they don't come back unless they have, like, a meeting or something that they have to attend. So like, not seeing him for the rest of the day is not, like, an un-normal thing.

Q: Okay.

A: Like - but, like, I'm saying, like, we don't really - the only reason we interact was kind of, like, by an off-chance thing. Like, I don't work with him.

Q: Mm-hm.

A: Um, so he, uh - yeah. We talked, like, randomly throughout the day, but it was really sporadic, and he seemed pretty busy. So we didn't talk too much. Like I said, didn't put too much thought into it. It happens all the time. Um, waited 'til about 3:45, then sent that text to me. And, yes, he does know that I will be home at that point, or getting home. Like...

Q: Did you give (Mark) (Jim)'s information?

A: No. I would really, like, not like to involve him in this.

Q: Okay.

A: He does not know about this. He didn't - and he was not - like, he doesn't know any of this is occurring.

Q: Okay.

A: Like, I was literally tryin' to...

Q: So he - he knows, certainly, through the media that somethin's occurred?

A: Yeah.

Q: With...

A: He's, like, out of town.

Q: ...Chris.

A: He's probably has no idea.

Q: Okay.

A: He doesn't know...

Q: Okay.

A: ...who Chris is. Like, he's not - I do not - no.

Q: So he's just a friend of yours...

A: Yes.

Q: ...um, that was...

A: He does not need to be dragged into this.

Q: ...coming to your apartment and doesn't know anything about Chr- does he know anything about Chris?

A: No.

Q: Okay.

A: Nothin'. Absolutely nothin'.

A1: Yeah. We've known (Jim) for...

A: He - yeah.

A1: ...ye- years and years.

A: Yeah.

Q: You're not datin' him or anything like that?

A: No.

Q: He's just a friend?

A: He's, like, one of my very good friends. Like, my dad knows him. He's a great guy. He just - he - he works out of state a lot. So when he's in town, um, we hang out. But when he's in town and he's off of work, to save time - I - so I - I gave him a key to my house one, 'cause I trust him and he's one of my best friends, and two, 'cause, uh, sometimes he will just meet me there. Because I'll be, like, "Hey, I'm gettin' off of work." And then if I get stuck in traffic or something, he ends up, like, sitting outside of my apartment waiting for me to get off of work. So I'm like, "Here's a key." And, like, my dog loves him and stuff. So no.

Q: Okay.

A: He's not involved with it...

Q: So he's just a family friend?

A: Yes. I don't even want him dragged...

Q: The only reason I ask...

A: ...into this.

Q: A- and I'm not really concerned, uh, about your location. Um, I think we already have your cell phone records. Um, at some point, i- did (Mark) ask you to supply - uh, did they ask for consent to get cell phone records. That'll probably be done by warrant, if we...

A: Isn't that what you just did?

Q: Nope. What I'm talkin' about is your movement.

A: Oh.

Q: Um, by GPS or by cell phone tower. To show where you were. Obviously - and I don't want to cause you concern. We want to know where you were that day, too. You're dating a man who did some egregious stuff, and we want to put - we want to show that you were never near him that day, period.

A: Oh, I mean, you guys can...

Q: So…

A: …track my stuff.

Q: No, i- I mean, that - that was somethin' we will have to get a warrant for, anyways, to - I'm just saying if - if we asked for it, would you have any objections…

A: Yeah, you're…

Q: …to that?

A: No. You can have it.

Q: All right. So, um, we'll…

A: I'm - I'm a pretty boring person. I don't…

Q: Well, it sounds like…

A: …go too many places.

Q: …you just went to work that day and then you came home and you were there at 3:45.

A: Yeah, like, give or take…

((Crosstalk))

A: …like, five minutes.

Q: Yeah. Right.

A: But yeah. So 3:45 I meet (Jim) there. Yeah, I would totally do…

Q: And so (Jim) is a - understand from an investigative point, he could be a person who could say, "Yeah. I was there at 3:45. I don't"

- he doesn't know Chris. He doesn't know anything. He could say, with one phone call, "Yeah, she came in at 3:45." Done.

A: Totally.

Q: Do you know what I'm sayin'?

A: Yeah.

Q: And I don't have to ask anything more than, "Hi, Chris. My name's Kevin. I'm..."

A: Oh.

Q: Or - or - or (Jim).

CHAPTER 9

The Missing Chapter

"The belief in a supernatural source of evil is not necessary. Men alone are quite capable of every wickedness."

By: Criminal Minds, Gideon

Why I believe there was involvement by NK in my book *The Murders of Christopher Watts*. I left a chapter out of my book. At the time, I felt I should not get involved with it. However, I am going to share that chapter with you now. Please understand that this is my theory after much research and conferring with others. I feel most of this can 100 percent be backed up; this is the "Missing Chapter" that was supposed to be in *The Murders of Christopher Watts:* Was There a Dark Spirit? After the sentencing and months after Christopher was in prison, some things have surfaced to cause me to pause and take notice. I think some things can maybe prove there was some dark activity going on. Suppose you take a man who has been completely passive and easygoing in his life by all who know him and think he's great (including his wife). How is it explained that over the course of a few weeks, he changes into a monster, unleashes the most horrific act possible, and kills a pregnant wife and two little daughters? Does it happen like that, or is there more to it?

Through research, I have found some very interesting information about NK. The FBI may already know these things.

However, since Christopher confessed, they didn't need to look further. From the beginning, he protected her with all of his might. If the FBI knows these things about her, they did not bring it public. I feel we did not see all of her interviews, and it's possible they found out more and didn't feel it had anything to do with the murders. I'm sure NK did not tell them she was making mind-altering drinks for him. Drinks that possibly could control his mind. Let me explain.

After you read this information, decide for yourself if it has anything to do with what Christopher did. If you think she was involved in any way. Listen, I am in no way implying that Christopher is innocent. He had a choice to make; he murdered his family. However, was his mind altered? Nikki was involved in a movement called *Gaia worship—the new pagan religion*. You can find more on this at enviomentcology.com. Nichole Kissinger had a business in Aurora, Colorado, called Satya Consulting LLC at Aurora Ave. Aurora, Colorado, this is a fact. Christopher said he knew nothing about this business. Follow me here—Satya is a company based on an Indian guru named Sathya Narayana Raju; he created the cult and claimed to be god. He supposedly performed miracles and claimed he was omnipresent, claimed he could heal, and all of these disasters that he could make happen because he was recruiting all these cult members; this became a trend across Colorado for the 20-30-somethings. Christopher knew enough to know it was very popular. Satya is a very important concept and virtue in Indian religions. Satya means "Truth," but the Latin word is "Satan." In Greek mythology, the word Satya means Satan. This cult is all over the world being used as "counseling," where they brainwash and hypnotize their clients until they are broken down so they can build them up to be a cult member and recruit others. Keep in mind NK had this counseling business.

You may find it interesting that just three days after the murders and Christopher had talked to the FBI, NK suddenly closed her business. We do not know if she closed it because she didn't want to be found out or if she was trying to avoid media attention, and of course, there could be another reason, but it is odd. Did she not want them to know she made drinks for Christopher to drink? Christopher said he was unaware of what she was into but knew she kept many things from him. Interestingly, he told me she had crystals all over her house. He said she would not go anywhere without some of her crystals. She collected crystals. He was not aware of why, but I believe it was for much more of a reason than he thought.

Christopher recalled that when they were in the mountains, she would take out a crystal, hold it toward the sky, and chant. When he questioned her about what she was doing, she said she was talking to her grandmother, who had passed on. He recalled in the mountains, she would disappear for hours. He didn't know what she was doing during that time. I asked Christopher if he was searching for a diamond for NK. Discovery said he was searching for diamonds on the internet. He says he never looked for diamonds for NK; he was searching for a certain crystal she wanted.

There is a philosophy called Gaian, based on a symbolic relationship between earth and all living things: mind, body, and spirit. All three must be aligned to be complete. While yoga also centers around these tenets, yoga is a practice rather than a philosophy or religion. There is a branch of Gaian philosophy, which is a form of pagan religious practice similar to Wicca (witchcraft). We believe NK was a follower of this form of worship. "Mind" is often aligned with meditation. (Nikki would hike and disappear for hours.) Meditation is also chakra alignment; sometimes, drugs are used to attain enlightenment or "open up" the mind. Crystals are another common tool used in this New Age practice. (Nikki carries crystals with her at all times.). The crystals are energy tools used to manifest intentions. "Body" is healed with a macro diet and fasting (all of which Nikki did). "Spirit" is aligned with channeling dreams, channeling spirits healing through energy, and Kundalini Awakening. These are just a few examples. If you experience an awakening, it is an intense physical and mental experience. It can be an emotional breakthrough, but it can also unearth deeply buried emotions or past experiences held deep within the psyche.

What happens when our kundalini awakens? If Kundalini is awoken, the energy is said to rise from the base of the spine from the root chakra, which in the parable has been referred to as the base of the mountains. The energy ascends to the peak, which correlates with the crown chakra and the pineal gland. When the pineal gland is activated, a major change in consciousness is experienced. (Carrellas, author of Urban Tantra) "Be aware and know the signs and symptoms of Kundalini awakening, and be aware of the changes that may occur so that you have spiritual practices and the support of masters to guide you through."

How to awaken your Kundalini energy.

Open your sushumna nadi and cease thinking.

According to Dr. David Frawley, "the awakening of Kundalini requires that life force enters into the sushummar central channel; this occurs when the prana is withdrawn from its fixation through the thought process on the external world"—*this may cause spiritual distress and a total breakdown, resulting in a major crisis.* Some people lose jobs and relationships; others experience difficult emotions from a traumatic past, as if the trauma is being relived at the moment. The test is if they can overcome and learn from the past or be beaten by the same demons from an earlier time. If you are well trained and guided, with strong and steady spiritual practices, you are more likely to manage the astonishing changes and sensations. It is sensible to follow a particular path, be trained to know the signs and symptoms of Kundalini Awakening, and be aware of the changes that may occur.

Take heed: awakening may not be contained.

Suppose a practitioner is unprepared or the Kundalini awakens spontaneously. In that case, there can be an experience of total chaos due to changes in motivation, appearance, diet, weight gain or loss, sensations in the crown of the head, and shifts in the personality that an unguided or unprepared person may not be able to handle. A spontaneous arousal of Kundalini energy can happen as a result of intense energy work, drug use, sexual experiences, abuse or trauma, yoga practices, or life events—Explains Dr. Grant.

Warning: subtle body awakening is in progress.

A kundalini awakening is not so much a physical force but the energy of the movement of the subtle body. If you are not rightly prepared, a kundalini awakening might cause a ruckus that might feel like a breakdown. Take caution as you explore the awakening of the serpent energy within you.

We do know by Christopher's account of the things that happened that NK was getting him ready for something. Why was she doing this? My belief is that she had opened a business prematurely. She had not had proper training and was unsure what she was doing. We also know that she would give Christopher these drinks called Devil's Breath. Telling Christopher they were a type of cleanse. He told me he did not know what was in them. He questioned if they could have had drugs in them because there were times he had a loss of memory or would seem to "wake up" and not remember what he was doing; also times, he would seemingly "blackout" and wake up and continue the sentence he had started. Was this a trance or a hypnosis? An article I read states you can use dioptase to open you up for preparation for 'awakening.' At times, he would complain of stomach pain. I also read that if you open a portal, you can't control what comes out. Remember this Kundalini was a service her friend offered in their business. Again, I do not believe NK knew what she was doing and was possibly practicing on Christopher.

Recipe for Devil's Breath Drink: 1/3 oz of Vodka, 1/3 ounce of Limoncello, 1/6 oz of Campari Bitters. You can mix it with different things, tomato juice, fruit juice, etc. Christopher says all he can remember is the drink was red.

Devil's Breath: Urban Legend or the World's Most Scary Drug?

In the past, there were stories circulating that a chemical known as "Devil's Breath" was making its way around the world, being blown into faces and soaked into business cards to render unsuspecting tourists incapacitated. The result? A "zombie-like "state that left victims with no ability to control their actions, leaving them at risk of having their bank accounts emptied, homes robbed, organs stolen, or raped by a street criminal. But are these sensationalized stories part of an urban legend or a factual crime scene?

Devil's Breath is derived from the flower of the "borrachero" shrub, common in the South American country of Columbia. When powdered and extracted via a chemical process, the seeds contain a chemical similar to scopolamine called "burandamga', Borrachero has been used for hundreds of years by native South Americans in spiritual rituals. The compound leads to hallucinations, frightening images, and a lack of free will. Amnesia can occur, leaving the victim powerless to recall events or identify perpetrators.

According to a 1995 Wall Street Journal article, about half of all emergency room admissions in Bogota, Colombia, were for burundanga poisoning. Scopolamine is also present in Jimson Weed, a plant that is found in most of the continental U.S. This drug is available in prescription form also. If you suffer from seasickness, maybe you've used scopolamine on your last ocean adventure. The active ingredient is available in a one-milligram transdermal patch worn behind your ear to help ward off nausea and vomiting. The medicine slowly absorbs through the skin from specialized rate-controlling membranes found in the patch. It's worn for three days before being replaced; this is usually given in a very low dose and prevents side effects in most people. Any dosage of this drug, or if used to spike drinks, could cause serious issues. The State Department mentions on its website that scopolamine can render a victim unconscious for 24 hours or more. In Columbia, where its use seems most widespread, "unofficial estimates" of scopolamine events are roughly 50,000 per year. In large doses, it can cause respiratory failure and death. However, these effects are due to oral administration of the drug, primarily in drinks. I find this very suspect, and I think the possibility that Christopher was given a drink that could have caused him to have hallucinations or memory loss is very likely. Those who have read my books or watched my interviews on television know I am not for Christopher. I hate what he did, and it makes him a monster, but I do believe this has to be looked at as a possibility.

CHAPTER 10

Mt. Theory

"Unfortunately, a superabundance of dreams is paid for by a growing potential for nightmares."

By: Sir Peter Ustinov

So, let's go with this theory for a moment. In my theory, I try to deliver the facts as I have found them and tell my readers that. Sometimes, I might interject my feelings but try really hard to stay on course and deliver what I know to be true. So here I go—the following is what I believe happened in the Watts case.

Christopher and Shanann were not happy in their marriage. As with all marriages, you may go through a slump. It's a day-to-day routine, not a lot of excitement. It is very hard to work every day, pay bills, meet all obligations, take care of the children, clean the house, cook meals, and do laundry. Sounds exciting, right? NOT. Shanann and Christopher were buried in bills and living way beyond their means. I do believe this was mostly Shanann's doing. He told me she wanted people to believe everything was perfect. She worked hard to keep that image. Looking from the outside in, they had it all. A beautiful home, two beautiful girls, a great car, and two beautiful people. Wow, who wouldn't want that? Christopher, that's who. Yet he never voiced his opinion about not being happy until very close to the end. Even then, he would tell Shanann he was going through something but would get over it. One time, he told me that he blamed the screens and too much Facebook time for causing them to go void. It was the ho-hum of you lay and watch your screen, and I'll lay and watch my screen, and never the twain shall meet.

He said when he tried talking to her, she was always so busy on her phone she didn't have time for him. However, this is how Shanann did her business. She had so many people under her with Thrive, and it took a lot to maintain. It took her day and night. Their marriage had grown cold. I believe Shanann thought the baby would give a spark back into their marriage, especially if it were a boy. Which we all know it was. So, is another baby an answer to boredom in your marriage? I believe not so much, but maybe the old Christopher would have felt differently about that. I do not believe he liked it when she put him on live, either. Which we know she often did and usually without notice. So, he resented her many hours of screen time. When he had something to say, she didn't care; she was focusing on her work, on Facebook, or her texts, usually until after 11 p.m. Christopher had to be up very early so he would fall asleep, and she would work as long as she needed to.

As great as their family looked on the outside, it was falling apart on the inside. Ready to implode, and the result is horrible. They had extreme financial problems. Christopher told me he used to feel so bad for how much Shanann worried about their finances. He said it was on her mind constantly. There was just not enough money to cover everything. It didn't have to be like that. She wouldn't hear of taking the girls out of a 25k-a-year school or downsizing their house. Think of how different the possibilities would have been for this family had they done those two things. Would he have still killed his family? I think yes. I say this because if he had met NK, I feel the outcome would still have been the same. I find myself saying sometimes, "Shanann, it could all be so different; hey girl, look at what's going on." However, we know that had this all not happened, we wouldn't know Shanann or anything she was going through. He would have been happy downsizing. But he never had that chance.

Instead of trying to explore their options, even if that had been a divorce, he took the awful road we all know he did; she knew it was inevitable but was trying to prevent having to give up all the material things and status that she felt others envied; this would show their friends they did not make enough money to pull it all off. It showed a flaw; I believe Shanann was so OCD that she would go to any extent to prove to others they were well off. They had filed for bankruptcy before, and he said they were heading for it again. Only it had not been long enough since the last time to file again. Obviously, they needed financial counseling; they needed marriage counseling. However, we know that was never given a chance.

Christopher and NK started an affair in early June of 2018. It started to escalate; Christopher was feeling pressured when he found out Shanann was pregnant. I do believe Christopher had decided with Shanann to have another baby. I know his mother was very much against the pregnancy, and Christopher also had that in mind. She usually did not get pregnant that fast, so that was a surprise for probably both of them. Shanann was elated, and I believe he would have been had he not been having an affair. She wanted so much to give him a boy and was on pins and needles until their ultrasound. She had hoped it would help the way he was feeling, and maybe their marriage would improve. I also believe that NK was pushing him. He told me that he felt like he was standing between Shanann and NK and was being pulled in both directions. He knew he had a choice; he just made the wrong one. That fatal mistake took him down the road to the most horrific thing imaginable. I know he is looking back at that decision now and regrets he ever allowed it to go this far. That's his regret, I think, more than the fact that he lost his precious three children and beautiful wife. He says he looks back and cannot believe he did something like this.

That's one reason why my theory may be the right theory. The real story, as we were talking about in his words, was "the night of." He looks back and feels like there was something that was over him. As he described this to me and his eyes turned black, I knew that the chills that were running up my spine and made a tingle on the top of my head, were from the words of a man that were reliving what he had done. It is my belief that NK was so desperate to have Christopher for herself that she gave him this drink called "Devil's Breath" to help her convince him to get "rid" of his family. Now, before you start shouting, "I knew it!" Let me explain what I mean. I feel she worked on him very hard the last few weeks before he left for North Carolina and even the week he came home. With the last night being the evening of Saturday, August 11, 2013. Telling him to get rid of Shanann and telling him to get rid of the family, but meaning it as to leave her or to leave his family.

I feel that when NK found out he had murdered his family in order to be with her, she was frightened and in total horror! However, I believe she realized it was because of what she was saying to him. I think she just could not believe her ears but realized he had taken her very literally. I do not believe she ever told him to kill or harm his family in any way, just meaning to leave them. Christopher is so simple-minded and has always been told by a woman what to do that he did not think twice, but to rid himself of all responsibility and get "rid" of his family, interpreted as murdering his family. I think for him, the most logical thing to do was to rid himself physically of his family and start all over. That's why he could tell me the thought of him ever being caught never entered his mind. He was following orders. I know it's a theory, but I do not believe I am wrong; this is why NK wanted to go to the police right away and tell them her whole side of everything and did not ever want to admit she may have been the one to have caused this. How scary and how totally horrible she had to have felt. She knew Christopher loved her, and she made sure he would do anything to please her. No, I don't think she would ever have wanted him to hurt his family. NEVER. As much as we don't like her, I don't think she is capable of that. I know some of you have said she did some bad things before, but this is totally a different level.

Please understand that this is my theory after much research and conferring with other people. I do feel most of this can 100 percent be backed up. My belief is the drinks that Christopher talked about were probably Devil's Breath. He would tell me how he would feel after being given these drinks. She was telling him she was giving him cleanse drinks. There were times after these drinks that he was unable to recall his time. He told me these things not long after the murders. He did not understand at that time what all of that meant. He said NK was so dark, and her spirit was so satanic that he knew it was where he picked up a dangerous dark spirit.

In the beginning, I think we all believed it was just part of his blaming the murders on something else. I no longer believe that. Here are my thoughts on this. I believe NK kept asking him to get rid of his family. In his mind, he conjured up a way to murder them, but I believe she meant for him to divorce Shanann. (get rid of her.) Honestly, as dark as she may be, I don't really believe she knew he was going to kill his family. However, I believe he is right, and he picked up something dark that entered his mind. Let's think about what this drink can do to people. Plus, if she was practicing her religious rituals. I don't believe she knew what she was doing and may have called up some evil spirits not really experienced with doing some of these things. Some of you may not believe this can happen. However, I completely believe there is something as dark and evil as dark spirits. Christopher talked about her religious beliefs and how dark she was. He told me very early on he felt he had been possessed with something. I put that in my book, *The Murders of Christopher Watts*, but did not really give much attention to it. Now, I do believe it, not for one second, giving that as an excuse but as a reason, possibly. *Please understand this does not mean in any way that he is not responsible for shanann and the girl's murders. He is totally and solely responsible, and he is a monster!*

If NK had him controlled by what she was doing to him when giving him drinks, I think she told him to get rid of his family. Again, not meaning murder, but to ensure he would tell Shanann he wanted a divorce. She knew he was afraid of Shanann, and this was the encouragement and nerve he needed. She thought she could build the nerve in him, I believe. From the very beginning, he told me things were foggy for him. I guess I assumed it was from all the trauma he had gone through. Most were self-induced trauma, but trauma still. NK had weeks to work on him, and I believe she took the opportunity. What was her end game? I'm not sure other than she wanted to see if she could make him leave his wife for her. Maybe she did intend they would divorce, and she and Christopher could build a life together. Maybe she even intended to be a stepmother to his girls. However, I don't believe she ever intended to be a stepmother to his children. She wanted to be the one to give him his first son. What does that say? You decide; law enforcement never looked any further.

CHAPTER 11

The Judge's Statement

"The bitterest tears shed over graves are for words left unsaid and deeds left undone."

By: Harriet Beecher Stowe

Below, I want you to read the in-pack statements and what the DA had to say about the case and Christopher. I write these letters as they were spoken. I'm sure they were nervous and emotional when they wrote these letters under great duress.

TAKEN FROM THE ACTUAL SENTENCING HEARING…..

VICTIM IMPACT STATEMENTS

<u>FRANKIE RZUECK:</u>

Shanann, Bella, CeCe loved people. They always had good times; this year was the first time they had gone to the beach, and they loved it. God only knows what happened that night. Our life will never be the same without Shanann, Bella, CeCe, and Nico. They had all their lives to live, and they were taken by the heartless one; this is the heartless one, the evil monster. How dare you take the lives of my daughter Shanann, Bella, Cece, and Nico. I trusted you to take care of them, and they also trusted you, and then you kill them. The heartless monster, and then you take and throw them out like trash. You disgust me. They were loving and caring people. You may have taken their bodies from me, but you will never take their love from me. They loved us more than you will ever know. Because you don't know what love is, because if you did, you would never have taken them from me—you monster.

You thought you would get away with this. I don't know how the cameras do not lie. You took them out of the house. Yes, I seen the videotape. You buried my daughter and Nico in a shallow grave; then you put Bella and Celeste in crude oil, you heartless monster. You have to live with this vision every day the rest of your life, and I hope you see them every time you close your eyes. Oh, I forgot, You have no heart, or feelings, or love. I will think of them every day of my life, and I love them every day of my life. Prison is too good for you; this is hard to say. I hope you enjoy your new life; it's nothing like the one you had before. May the courts have no mercy on you. It's hard. It hurts in so many ways. I have heard people say you're not a monster; no, you're an evil monster. Thank you, Shanann, Bella, Cece, and Nico. Papa loves you. One other thing: Shanann says she is super excited to get justice today.

FRANKIE RUZECK JR.: STANDING WITH THE D.A. WHILE HIS LETTER IS READ

Your Honor, the past three months, I have hardly slept because I have been going through a lot of emotions because I did not see this coming. You went from being my brother my sister's protector. One of the most loved people in my family, too, someone who I will spend the rest of my life trying to understand. What gives you the right to put your hands on a woman, let alone my best friend, my sister, and your daughters? Why weren't they enough for you? In a blink of an eye, you took away my whole world, the people I loved most in my life. They trusted; they loved you. They looked up to them because you promised to keep them safe. The people I loved, my sister, your daughters, and son. You turned on your family.

My blood is boiling as I say these last words because they are the last you will ever hear from me. I can't even think of the words to describe the betrayal. And to be honest, you aren't even worth the time It takes to put pen to this paper. There isn't a day that goes by that I don't cry for my family; they were my whole world. All I do is ask myself why. Why would you do this? You don't deserve to be called a man. What kind of person slaughters his whole family, the people who loved him the most? Did you really think you'd get away with this? That this was your best option to throw away your family like they were garbage. They deserved better, and you know it. I hope you spend the rest of your life staring at the ceiling at night and being haunted for what you've done. None of us deserve this.

Hearing my mother and father cry themselves to sleep in their hotel room hurts more than you know. I can't describe how badly this makes me feel for my poor parents. We trusted you. You have taken away my family from this earth, but you can never take them away from my heart. You took away my privilege of being called uncle. to the most precious little girls. I will never be called uncle again. But you will never be called daddy again, either. You will never be able to put your hands on another woman again, let alone my sister, my best friend. I just can't comprehend how they weren't enough for you. Shanann, Bella, and CeCe loved you more than anyone. You were their hero. How could you destroy the people who loved you the most? I pray that you'll never have peace or a good night's rest in the cage you will forever call your home you live in.

A cage you are privileged to live in because we begged the District Attorney to spare your life because, despite everything, we believe no one has the right to take the life of another—even someone like you. I feel sorry for your family. I feel sorry for the pain they must have that they can't hug you, like the pain my father, mother, and me have every time we cry for our family. Nothing hurts more than hearing my family weep for their loved ones. I just wish I could get you to tell the truth, but I know that is asking for more than you are capable of. I stayed up all night writing this letter; I don't know how my life can ever be the same anymore. My conscience is clear: I get to live free, but I can't say the same for you. I haven't slept in two days because I've been anxiously waiting for this moment. The moment I get to tell you how I feel. How this has affected my family and I. My family can finally grieve after today. If anything, we will come out of this stronger than ever before, and we will continue to pray for your family.

SANDY RZUECK:

Good Morning, your Honor; thank you for this moment. I want to take a moment to thank everyone who has prayed for our beloved family—the gifts and cards from all over the world. I know God will put the evil people where they need to be. I also want to take the time to thank the town of Fredrick. The DA's office, the CBI, the FBI for their exceptional work. We thank both Nicole Atkinson and Nate; they are the true heroes they really are. God Bless. God makes no mistakes as to who he puts in your life. Marriage is about love, trust, friendship, and unity. We marry for better or worse until death do us part. Our daughter Shanann loved you with all of her heart; your children loved you to the moon and back. Shanann's family was her world. Shanann put a crown on your head, but fortunately, the day you took their life, God removed that crown. We loved you like a son; we trusted you. Your faithful wife trusted you. Your children adored you, and they also trusted you. Your daughter Bella Marie sang a song about you. I don't know if you got to see it, but she sang Daddy, you're my hero. I have no idea who gave you the right to take their lives. But I know God and his mighty angels were there to bring them home to paradise. So not only did you take a family of four, your family of four, but you also took your own life. I want the world to know that our daughter and her children were so loved by us. There will always be protected by God and his mighty angels. I didn't want death for you because that is not my right. Your life is between you and God, and I pray he has mercy for you. From Shanann's mother, Bella, CeCe, and Nico's Nana. Thank you, your honor.

The Watts attorney, along with Cindy and Ronnie Watts, came front to make a statement. The attorney read the letter for Ronnie Watts; Cindy Watts wanted to read her own. On behalf of the Watts, your Honor, and to the community, we thank you for the opportunity. We come today as the Grandparents and the Daughters whose lives were taken in this case.

We are not here to ask for leniency; we are not condoning the conduct of the Crime that has occurred and pain that it has caused. We join our daughter-in-law's family in saying This should never have happened, this is not condonable, this is something we will never get over. We appreciate the consideration that has been given. Mostly the families that have lost everyone. We appreciate that they begged for Christopher's life. We agree and echo what they have said that it is not his place to take a life, nor would it be our place as a community to take his life. So, we thank you for the opportunity and every effort that has been put out in this case. The prosecution, in this case, has respected the Bill of Rights. They took the time to explain that the information we gave was not correct; they were misinformed. They did not intend to cause pain on anyone. They appreciate the prosecution to answer questions and take the time and consideration so that they could tell this court and the community that the interview content was not their message. They accept that their son has done this. They accept that he has decided to plead guilty, that they requested our agreement in a life sentence.

We appreciate that he is given the chance to serve a life sentence. It is his responsibility to serve that life's sentence. And it is not enough to make up for what has been done. We understand and join the family, and that we have questions. We don't know how such a thing could possibly happen or how a man who was responsible for his wife and children could take their lives and that he could disregard their bodies and the love he had for them and they had for him and everyone else. And put this community through having to bring justice. We do not understand that; we do not think it was appropriate and not begin to think there is an explanation that will ever justify it. They want everyone to know that a full confession with accountability has not occurred. They support the family in the request that that happens. If not today, in an appropriate time and manner so that everyone can have peace, so they can understand, and have their questions answered. So, to be given a life's sentence gives the opportunity he can have to give it. Had the death penalty been given, there would not have been the opportunity to be accountable and give a full confession. Had the death penalty been sought, the council would have fought for his life, and there would have been a multiple-year battle, and the community would have to subsidize it, and the family would have to endure it. We have so much respect and gratefulness that this did not happen. We encourage Christopher Watts, in the time he feels, to give an account of what happened with the guidance of his counsel. We feel it would be appropriate to heal their pain and suffering. But we also say we don't believe there is anything he can say to cure the harm that he has caused. He has the responsibility to serve his sentence with dignity with regard to everyone and to spend every breath he has left in atonement for what he has done.

CINDY WATTS:

My name is Cindy Watts; I am the grandmother of two beautiful granddaughters, Bella Marie and Celeste Kathryn Watts. I am also the mother of Christopher Watts, who I will be directing most of my letter to. First, I would like to address this crime and the horrible loss the Rzueck and our family has faced. Our heart has been broken by the needless deaths of Shanann, Bella, CeCe, and Nico; this is something we will never get over. We will mourn in the loss of our family, and in that, we are united in our grief. I am still struggling to understand how and why this tragedy occurred. I may never be able to understand, but I pray for peace and healing for all of us. Now, to my son Christopher, I have known you since the day you came into this world. I have watched you grow from a quiet and sweet, curious child who Bella reminded me of so much to a young man who worked so hard in sports and later in mechanics to achieve your goals. You are a good friend, father, and son. We have loved you from the beginning, and we still love you now. It might be hard for some to understand how we can tell you, although we can't imagine what could have led us to this day. We love you. Maybe you can't believe it either. As it's said in Jeremiah 31:3, "I have loved you with an everlasting love; therefore, I continue my faithfulness to you." And I always loved you and still do; your father, sister, and I are struggling to understand, but we will remain faithful to you just as God is faithful because of his unconditional love for all. We love you, and we forgive you son.

RONNIE WATTS:

My name is Ronnie Watts, and I am the grandfather of Bella, Celeste, and Nico Watts, and I am the father of Christopher Watts. One of the most important things I have done in my life is to raise my children and to watch as they have started their own families. I spent many years coaching Little League, talking to my son, and sharing my knowledge of cars. He was just as involved with his girls. I believe he loves his girls; I know he does. This tragedy has affected our families in so many ways. Beyond losing our precious granddaughters and our beloved daughter-in-law, we are forced to question everything. We don't have all the answers, and I hope one day, Christopher, you can help us. Chris, I want to talk to you as a father and son. You are here today accepting responsibility, but I want to tell you I love you. I forgive you. The Bible says if we ask, he is just to forgive us. I forgive you; your sister forgives you, and we will never abandon you, and we love you. Dad.

Before we get to the D.A.'s statement, I want to give my opinion on these letters. For me, it goes without saying that the Rzueck's letters were beyond heartfelt. I'm sure they had a hard time putting into words how they were feeling. There really are no words for what they were going through. Beautiful words by Sandi; you could feel her pain.

My opinion, where the Watts were concerned, I'm sure they were in pain. However, it is shallow to me. Just words, as they had spoken so badly of Shanann. Really disrespectful to their own grandchildren. I noticed his mother could not bring herself to saying anything good about Shanann. Her attempts to keep telling Christopher how much she loved him just kept piling on the hate she showed for Shanann. There is nothing wrong with standing by your son because he is your son, and you will always be his parents, but to me sickening as she carried on. None of it felt true. I know first-hand because she told me directly how much she hated Shanann.

THE D.A.'S COMMENTS:

Your honor, there are no words to adequately express my feelings today: The horror, the pain, or the suffering the defendant has caused these families, these communities, and to all that were a part of this investigation. However, I do want to share for a few minutes the details of the crime. The questions that have screemed out to anyone that would listen since August 13, 2018, are why and how. Why did this have to happen? How could a seemingly normal husband and father annihilate his entire family? These are the questions that only one person on this planet can answer. I fully expect we will not receive the answer to those questions today, nor will we in the future. I don't expect that he will ever tell the truth about what really happened or why. Even if he did, there is no way that any rational human being could find those responses and answers to those horrific actions. There is some kind of understanding from the evidence we have. And the evidence tells us the defendant coldly and deliberately ended four lives. Not in a fit of rage, not by accident, but in a calculating and sickening manner. Shanann was 34 years old when she married the defendant in November of 2012. Over the weekend leading up to August 13, she had been at a conference in Phoenix, Arizona. She returned home in the early hours of August 13. We know she got home about 1:45 in the morning; her camera on the doorbell shows her arriving back home from the airport. Shortly thereafter, at least according to the defendant, they had what he refers to an emotional conversation.

About the state of their marriage and about what their lives would look like going forward. What was said during that emotional conversation, only he knows. What we do know is shortly after that, the defendant then strangled her to death with his own hands. We know that he slowly took her life that morning; it was not done in a vengeful manner, as he told the CBI and FBI. Had it been that way, you would have seen horrible bruising in the neck, shoulders, and face. You would expect to see the highway bone in her neck broken. You would expect to see some kind of defense wounds on his body as she would have struggled and fought for her life. None of those are present. The only injuries that were on Shanann was fingernail bruising on the right side of her neck. Experts tell us it takes two to four minutes to strangle someone to death. The horror she felt as the man she loved wrapped his hands around her neck and choked the life out of her must have been unimaginable. Even worse, what must Bella, age four, and Celeste, age three must, have thought as their father, the one man on this planet, was snuffing out their lives? They from smothering. Let me say that again: the man sitting to my right smothered his daughters. What must Imagine the horror in Bella's mind as he snuffed out their life.

Your honor, Bella fought back; the frenulum in her mouth has a centimeter and a half tear. She bit her tongue multiple times before she died. She fought back for her life as her father smothered her. Celeste had no such injuries. In fact, she had no external injuries at all. But according to the medical examiner, she was smothered nonetheless. The defendant then methodically and calmly loaded their bodies into his work truck. Not in a hastily or disorganized way. He was seen from the neighbor's camera backing his truck into the drive and going back and forth into the house and into the truck three different times. One time for each of their bodies. He then drove them away from their family home one final time with the intent of hiding any evidence of the crime he had just committed. In one final sign of callousness for his wife, daughters, and unborn son and their remains, he drove them to a location in which no one would ever find them; he drove to an oil tank battery in which he is so familiar. He knew this was safe. He had texted a co-worker the night before, saying I'll head out to that site; I'll take care of it. He had assured he would be alone in the middle of the plains to get secretly get rid of his family's remains in a place he hoped they would never be found. One final measure of disrespect for the family he once had, he would assure they would not be together, even in death, or so he thought. He then put them in different locations. He buried Shanann and their unborn son in a shallow grave away from the oil tanks. Bella and Celeste were thrown away in oil tanks at this facility. Different tanks so these little girls would not be together even in death. Imagine this your horror: this defendant took these little girls and put them through an oil tank hatch barely eight inches in diameter. Bella had scratches on their buttocks from being shoved in this tank. A tuft of blonde hair was found on the hatch. The defendant said that Bellas' tank seemed emptier than that of CeCe's because of the sound that the splashes made. These were his daughters, your Honor. Significantly, when his co-workers arrived at the tanks later, he was described as acting normally.

It was a normal work day. Even as his daughters sank in the oil and water not far from him. Then, his deception truly really began. We've all seen the emotionless interviews of the defendant gives to the local media, asking for help in finding his family. We watched as he claimed the house was empty without them, and he hoped that they were somewhere safe, and he just wanted them to come home. He claimed that the girls were sleeping when he left that morning, and Shanann had told him she was taking them to a friend's house for the day. What is striking about this case, your honor, beyond the horrors I have described to you, is the number of collateral victims he collected. While he stood in front of a T.V. camera asking for the safe return of his family, scores of law enforcement officers, neighbors, friends, and family scoured the area, fretted for their safe return; they texted him begging for any information, sending him well wishes while all the while hiding what he had done. The list of victims does not end there; think of the Colorado firefighters and state patrol hazmat experts who had to dawn their protective suits that were called upon to pull Bella and Celeste out of those oil tanks. Or the Coroner employees that had to perform autopsies on these victims. Or the victim assistant frantically attempted to ease the suffering of these people who were affected. All of this, your honor, for what? Why? Why did this have to happen? His motive was simple—your honor. He had a desire to have a fresh start.

To begin a relationship with a new love that overpowered all decency and feelings for his wife and, daughters, and unborn son. While Shanann texted him over and over again in the days and weeks leading up to her death in an attempt to save her marriage. He secreted pictures of his girlfriend on his phone and texted her all hours of the day and night. While Shanann sent the defendant self-help and relationship counseling books, which, one ironically, was thrown in the garbage. He was searching the internet for secluded vacation spots to take his new love and researching jewelry. While

Shanann took the girls to visit the family in North Carolina, the defendant went to car museums and the sand dunes with his new girlfriend. The stark contrast between the subjects of their internet and text content is absolutely stunning. Even the morning after he killed them and disposed of their bodies, he made several phone calls. One was to the school where the girls were supposed to start. Telling them the girls would not be coming to unenroll them. Presumably, to give him more time before law enforcement notification about them going missing.

He contacted a realtor to discuss the selling of his house, and he texted his girlfriend about their future. None of this answers the questions as to why. If you are that unhappy, Get a divorce! You don't annihilate your family; throw them away like garbage. Why did Nico, Celeste, Bella, and Shanann have to lose their lives in order for him to get what he wanted? Your honor demands a maximum sentence under the agreement. As you recall, the agreement calls for life sentences for Shanann, Bella, Celeste, and all of those to run consecutively to one another. It also calls for the unlawful termination of pregnancy for Nico to run consecutively to counts one, two, and three. I would suggest that the extreme aggravation in the defendant's conduct and the efforts I have described to run consecutively to counts seven, eight, nine, tampering with a deceased human body, each be the maximum of twelve years, and for those to run consecutively to counts one, two, three. It is very clear this is not the result of one act. Each oil tank that he put his daughters in and the grave he dug for his wife mandate for these sentences to run consecutively. It's been alluded to that the defendant was eligible for the death sentence in this case. As you heard, Shanann's family strongly opposed to my office seeking the death penalty and being bound to the criminal justice system for the next several decades. That's in large part why we reached the penalty that we have. Four lives were lost on August 13 for reasons we will never understand or never know. In the end, the Rzueck family was much more merciful towards him than he was towards his wife, his daughters, and unborn son. Prison for the rest of his life is exactly where he belongs for the rest of his life.

The judge offered for Christopher to make a statement; however, Christopher declined.

THE JUDGE'S SENTENCE:

So, the court has considered the arguments made by the attorneys, and the court has considered the statements made by the victims in this case. The court finds that the plea agreement is fair and reasonable under the circumstances. I want to acknowledge the Rzuecks family, as well as the Watts family, that showing mercy on Mr. Watts is understood. I respect that and will accept the plea bargain under the circumstances.

Words that come to mind when I hear the evidence in this case are senseless in this crime and the viciousness of this crime. And equally aggravating in this court's determination is the despicable act of disposing of the bodies in which they were done in this case. I have been a judicial officer in the courts for seventeen years, and I will say this is perhaps the most inhumane and vicious crime that I have handled in the thousands of cases I have had. Anything less than the maximum sentence would depreciate the seriousness of this offense. So the court is going to sentence you as follows: As to count one murder in the first degree as it relates to Shanann Watts, the court is going to sentence you to a life sentence in the Colorado Department of Corrections with no possibility of parole. And that is going to run consecutively to all but counts three and four. With count two as it relates to murder in the first degree with Bella, I'm going to sentence you to a life sentence with no possibility of parole. As regard to count three as it relates to murder in the first degree to Celeste, I'm going to sentence you to life in prison without the possibility of parole. As to counts four and five as it relates to a different theory of murder in the first degree of Bella and Celeste to life in the Colorado prison as it relates to a different theory and is to run consecutively to counts one, two, three. The unlawful termination for an unborn child, the court believes the maximum of forty-eight years is appropriate. To be run consecutively. As to counts seven, eight, and nine as it relates to tampering of a deceased body, a class three sentence to run consecutively to the other counts. That will be the sentence of the court. Deputies, I would ask that you take this defendant and have him spend the rest of his life in the Department of Corrections. This was the end of the court sentencing for Christopher Watts.

I've never seen a man who had so much at such a young age and didn't realize what he had and just opened up the garbage can and threw them all away. Sidebar here: The day after the murders, August 14, an unexpected storm blew into his neighborhood. The wind blew in hard with some rain. When the storm was over, he looked outside, and a neighbor's three garbage cans had blown into Christopher's yard. He said as he stood there looking at them. The first thing he thought of was that I just threw my family away. I cannot imagine the horror you would feel for what you just did. Before his decision to murder his whole family, it's too bad he didn't take a step back and observe and appreciate all he had. I also want to say here the thought that Shanann killed the girls and he killed Shanann is as absurd as saying CeCe did it. Shanann, as a loving mother, wife, homemaker, and businesswoman, loved those kids with the whole of her heart. I'm very sure the thought of murder never entered her mind.

So, I'll get back to what I believe happened. NK, I believe, could sense at times the guilt Christopher was feeling over cheating on his family. So, she decided to step up her game. She offered him all sorts of elicited sex. Feeling this would pull him toward her, and it worked. Christopher said she would talk about Shanann a lot and ask him all sorts of questions. I believe she was obsessed with Shanann and wanted her life, her home. She did spend time over there, and the belief that she was only there twice is a total lie.

About the time Christopher was going to the Carolinas to meet Shanann and the girls, he started to feel less enamored toward NK. They stopped having sex so often, and he said at one point, he was even a little irritated when he wanted to go home for a while and wanted to just think about everything. She was afraid to let that happen because he might choose his family. So, she showed up at his house. He told me that was a fatal move because had she not been so aggressive toward him, he may have spent time in the house, looking at pictures, going through the home, and noticing all he had. Questioning himself, does he really want to give this all up? By this time, he was already planning in his head to kill his family, but he couldn't go to prison for life for thinking about it.

He told me he asked NK to give him the week he needed to spend with his family, and he would tell Shanann he wanted a divorce. He said he was at the airport when he got a text from NK saying she hoped he had a good time with his family and she would be waiting for him when he got back. That evening, she was texting him, "Are you with HER"? —Speaking of Shanann. Of course, he was with his wife and family. I believe NK hopped on a plane and went to North Carolina. I believe she was staying close to where Christopher and Shanann were vacationing. When he left at night, instead of talking to NK on the phone, I believe she was there, and he met with her in the evenings to have sex and to be pulled even more into her grips. Shanann wasn't given the same chance to fight for her husband and her family. She knew something was wrong, but he kept denying there was anyone else. During the day, they would go to the beach to play. One of my Facebook friends messaged me with a picture that looks like NK in the background as Christopher played on the beach with his family. If you've watched the videos of the family together, you will see that Christopher was obviously in a total funk. His head was somewhere else; you can watch as Shanann was trying. It's very sad.

Another event that was not helping their relationship was the big fight between Shanann and Christopher's parents. This complete story is in my book, *The Murders of Christopher Watts*. They argued over the fact that his mother gave the girls ice cream with nuts in it. CeCe was allergic to tree nuts. I asked Christopher if this was true because his mother told me it was not true. He said, "Yes, CeCe was allergic to tree nuts." She would break out in a rash and sometimes show difficulty in breathing. I'm not sure why his mother could not respect Shanann's wishes of not feeding her girls nuts. That is the mother's decision, not that of the grandmother. They got into a huge argument, and Shanann called her dad to come and get her. That is the last time the Watts saw their grandchildren. They left on bad terms. During the time Shanann and the girls were still in North Carolina, CeCe had a birthday party. The Watts were invited but did not attend. A pattern here.

The first day Christopher was in North Carolina, he visited his parents and sister. I was told it was there that while sitting on the front porch, his mother gave him the idea to write a letter that stated something like, "If something happens to me, you need to look at my wife, Shanann." Such an odd thing, don't you think, that his mother would do that? Also, during that visit, he told his parents about NK. He told them that he and Shanann were going to be getting a divorce—a win for the Watts side.

That night, before they went to bed, Christopher fixed a *Thrive* drink for Shanann. He put several crushed-up oxy tablets in her drink. He thought enough to make her miscarriage. I can tell you that is not something he thought of himself to do. So, where did Christopher get the Oxy? I do not believe he brought them with him to North Carolina. Shanann did not use Oxy. She did not have oxy at home in the basement, as some tried to say. It is simply not true. To cause a miscarriage was never in his plans until now. Remember, I believe NK came to North Carolina; then there was also his family. He went to the nursing home to see his grandmother, or did he meet someone completely off-record that we don't know about? Fortunately, it did not work. Shanann spent a lot of the night throwing up, very sick. Christopher told me Shanann's brother stayed up with her and helped her while she was sick. Christopher could not offer one bit of comfort or help that night; he was very cold-hearted.

Christopher, Shanann, and the girls flew home on August 6, 2018. I can't help but think about Shanann and those girls being just seven days from their death. So, heart-wrenching. The little girls are happy, enjoying their plane ride back to their doom. What a horrible thought. During the week after they got home, Shanann felt Christopher was warming up a little. She said they were able to talk some, and she felt maybe there was hope. They did have one huge fight where she threw him out of the bedroom and told him whomever he was with she hoped it was worth it.

So, it's very unfortunate that those little girls left this world under these circumstances. My opinion is the hatred that came from the Watts side did not need to be there. The constant control that was put on Shanann, she was not the type to give into that. I don't think even her mother would have gotten away with the total disregard for parenting. It's really awful that when Shanann and the girls died, there was never any healing between them. I do believe that to make Christopher happy, Shanann was willing to try; she sent a picture of the ultrasound that showed they were having a boy to the Watts.

Over the few weeks since the argument between his mother and Shanann, she was very angry and insisted Christopher do something about it. He did talk to his mother, but as many times before, I don't think it carried much weight. After they got home, Shanann had an appointment to have an ultrasound. Christopher was to leave work and meet her at the clinic where she was having her ultrasound. He was late because he stopped by NK's apartment. It's Very sad; Christopher would not even hold Shanann's hand during the ultrasound. All he felt was anger and resentment. He did not want the baby. It was very hurtful for Shanann.

There was a reveal party planned for that week. Things were so bad between them that Shanann canceled the party. She opened the envelope with the results. It's a boy! She was very excited and texted Christopher to let him know. It seemed to touch him some. He thought back to the day NK came to his house; they were talking about Shanann's pregnancy. NK told Christopher she wanted to give him a boy. She was very jealous of Shanann's pregnancy.

I have to pause here and think how horrible it was for Shanann that week, the ache in the pit of her stomach. The hours that went by that Christopher was working, and she could only text him. He wouldn't answer. She had no answer as to why he was so distant, why he had changed. He wasn't being truthful, and she could feel it. Why had this gentle, kind husband changed so much? Had she been too bossy, too demanding of him? Was it because of his parents? Should she make amends? All of these questions must have gone through her head. It must have been hard even to function. It is said she was not even on Facebook as much anymore. The problems were huge. The weight of her marriage, the finances, and the children for a pregnant mother must have been almost too much to carry.

It was the week Shanann had to go to Phoenix for a Thrive conference. It was important for her to be there. They gave awards, and they learned of new products and upcoming incentives. Things were so bad at home that she was willing to cancel her trip. She talked to Christopher about canceling, and he told her to go and that they would talk when she got back home. At the conference, her friends said she was acting "off." She was worried, but she shared some of her concerns with them. That sick punch in the stomach feeling, I believe, stayed with her all weekend. Maybe deep down, her soul knew something really bad was about to happen; however, I don't believe being murdered by Christopher ever crossed her mind.

CHAPTER 12

Last Time He Tucked His Babies In

"**Evil is unspectacular, and always human, and shares our bed and eats at our table.**"

By: W.H. Auden

When I went to the Dr. Oz show, I met Melissa Moore. Her father was the Happy Face Killer. She and I have remained friends. She told me through everything she had been through that it's very typical for these murderers to think they are so much smarter than everyone else, and they play mind games with us. I learned that's what Christopher was doing to me, and since then, I have seen how he plays mind games with many women who write to him. Some believe him so much that they will defend him to me. It's interesting how women who write to him will message me to let me know and see what I think about their correspondence with him. They all believe he has changed and are telling them the truth now until they realize he isn't. He knows how to play them and causes them even to feel sorry for him; he is a player. Many of these women will send him money.

As Shanann is at the airport trying to get home to her family on August 12, Christopher is in a very evil and dark mood and is laying his daughters down for the night with plans to take their lives once they are asleep. He reads them bedtime stories, covers them up, and kisses them goodnight, thinking *this will be the last time I will tuck my babies into bed.*

Feeling the darkness in him rise as if it were going to erupt any moment, he lay on his and Shanann's bed, waiting to know the girls were sound asleep. He had spent over an hour on the phone with NK. We don't know what this conversation consisted of, but in my opinion, I think NK made it very clear for Christopher to get rid of Shannan once and for all. A man used to doing what he is told by the women in his life weighed out the difference of his life without Shanann and the girls, or just without Shanann. I believe they argued as she gave him all the reasons it made sense to leave Shanann. I have no doubt Christopher paced the floors, waiting for Shanann to get home and working up the nerve to kill his family. As his little girls slept, their daddy, who was their world, was making plans to take their lives, and he did so in a brutal, horrible way.

He quietly laid on the bed, hearing Shanann come into the house. Pretending to be asleep, she slipped into the bed and under the sheet. She laid her hand on his leg, needing reassurance from this man she loved and adored—the father of her three children.

He took the touch of her hand as a signal to have sex. He turned over and began to make love to her. At that moment, she was thinking things were better than they had been. He was thinking about how he needed to check one last time if he felt anything for Shanann or if he only wanted NK. Unfortunately for Shanann, he didn't feel what he should have for her. After having sex with her, he watched her as she fell asleep. He then slipped out of bed and into Cece's room. He held a pillow over her face and put all of his weight on top of her. He felt her little body go limp, and her lips looked blue. She was gone (or at least he thought). No breath came out of her nose; her chest was not moving. *She's gone; this was easier than he thought.*

He quietly moved to Bella's room, small little Bella, his firstborn, his princess. He took a pillow and repeated the same thing again. Now, feeling sure of himself, the darkness moved him back to Shanann. She felt him get back in bed and told him she loved him. He didn't return her feelings, and she immediately asked him why. He expressed his dislike for the constant arguments she had with his parents, then demanded he intervene and make his parents apologize to her. He told her he wasn't going to do that any longer.

She became angry and told him his parents would never see the children again. He slipped his hands around her neck and got on top of her. She told him to be careful and not hurt the baby. He thought that she believed he was going to have sex with her again, but instead, he started squeezing her neck tighter and tighter until he couldn't stop. Surprisingly, she did not fight back. He says he held his hands there for four to five minutes until he knew she was gone. He remembers that she relieved herself, and he knew she had died. Right before he saw life leave her, he told her he did not love her anymore. He remembers her mascara running down her face. He wonders why her mascara streaking down her face is something he remembers and thinks about how she always washed her makeup off before coming to bed. One comment he made to the FBI is sickening to me. The FBI asked him what he thought Shanann was thinking as he was killing her. He replied, "She was probably thinking, *Lord, forgive him because he knows not what he is doing.*" That is a very offensive thing to say. I assure you that is not what she was thinking.

At that point, he felt the strong presence of evil that had weighed down on him release him from its grasp. Shanann had soiled the sheets on their bed; he rolled her off onto the top sheet as he heard Bella walk into the room. "Daddy, what's wrong with mommy?" He said he was so unbelievably shocked that Bella was awake. He noticed she had a black bruise above her eye. He said she looked like she had been through something. He knew she had died and came back, and he didn't understand what had happened. He told Bella Mommy was sick and they were going to take her to the hospital. About that time, Cece came into the bedroom. It horrified him! How could this be? He said he was beside himself.

Christopher was frantic and did not know what to do. He says he decided at that moment to load everyone in his truck and take them to Cervi. If you'd like to read this confession for yourself, a copy of his letter where he confesses this to me is in my book, *The Murders of Christopher Watts*. Christopher said he feels like God gave him three chances to turn around and not do this. One of those chances, he says, is when the girls woke up. God gave him a chance to turn this around. However, there was so much evil in him wanting to come out that he could only hear one thing: NK telling him to get rid of his wife so they could be together.

The trip down the stairs felt very overwhelming. The girls were watching and crying. Cece seemed there was something very wrong. He thought to himself that she might be almost dead. She seemed to wander around, almost like she didn't know where she was. Was this from what he had done to her or because it was the middle of the night? I believe she was suffering from severe brain damage at this point.

He struggled with Shanann's body and dragged her down the stairs. Listening to the thump as her body hit each stair. He knew this was very bad, but he felt a rage inside of him that he had not felt before. A rage because the girls had woken up and messed up his whole plan. He pulled Shanann's body through the garage and wrestled with getting her onto the floor of his truck. He went to the other side to pull her body through. As he walked back to the driver's side, he saw the girls moving his way.

Now, I'm not sure that NK wasn't with him at this point. There have been many videos released where we can see what seems to be her standing in the driveway behind his truck. Again, I don't believe she killed the girls, but I think she was aware of it that morning and maybe even helped him get rid of their bodies.

He lifted both of the girls into his truck. They huddled together, whimpering. He ran back inside and down to the basement and grabbed a couple of garbage bags. He put one over Shanann's head and one over her feet. The girls kept asking him what the smell was, but he didn't answer.

As he pulled out of the driveway, he had so much anger against the girls. He didn't understand why or how they had to wake back up. He was worried about the amount of time he had instead of the fact that his baby girls were crying as they sat with their dead mommy under their feet. With only a few minutes left to live, he gave no consoling to his babies. He just felt anger for them being alive.

About forty-five minutes later, he pulled into Cervi; he rolled Shannan's body onto the ground. He says he started digging a grave as fast as he could while the girls remained in the backseat of his truck. He said he remembered they were crying, Cece whimpering. The girls had no idea what was happening. Yet Bella was old enough to know something terrible was going on, and she had no strength to stop her dad, her hero, her murderer. Once a shallow grave was dug, he said he pulled the sheet and let Shanann roll into the grave, not caring how she would land. As he looked down on her body, he noticed she had given birth to their son. However, he was unaffected by what he saw. He discards the sheet in the field close to him. He said he then proceeded to kill the girls. He took Cece first; she was easy, no fight. The poor baby died at the hands of her father as he squeezed the life out of her. He had no feelings, no regret, just rid himself one by one of the family he brought into this world.

As Bella watched in horror, Christopher walked up to the first oil battery. Cece went quickly, so he didn't spend much time. No kisses goodbye, no "Daddy loves you," just literally cramming her through an eight-inch hole. Take your dinner plate. It's probably eight inches or ten inches in diameter. Think of being able to stuff a child through that hole. I can't help but wonder if she was dead when he put her through that hole. He told me he put them in the batteries so they wouldn't wake up again. I know there are people who do not believe he did this, but I assure you he did. He recalled with vivid memory at the time, although now he will say he does not clearly remember.

He says after he was done with Cece, he walked back to his truck. Poor little Bella was crying and saying, "Daddy, are you going to do to me what you did to Cece? Imagine the horror in that little girl as she couldn't get an answer from her daddy. Instead of being loving and consoling to his little girl, he put his hands around her head and mouth and smothered her. She fought him with everything she had in her, so much so that she died a violent and painful death. In my opinion, this put Christopher in another class all by himself. The brutal and unfeeling way he caused his baby girl to suffer is unimaginable for most. Can this possibly be just because he had a mistress? Again, my opinion is there is more to this story.

Let's look at my theory and say NK was with him; she followed him to Cervi. He had killed his babies, and maybe she stood by, or maybe she helped dig Shanann's grave while watching in horror as the man she claimed to love was doing something so monstrous. Did she carry one of the girls up the steps of the oil batteries? Did she walk one of them to the top, and then Christopher took over from there? I do believe without any doubt that Christopher took his foot and stomped Bella through the hole, so this is the part I'm not sure of: Was NK with him at Cervi, or did she head home in horror from the house? Realizing what she had done—created a monster. Not believing what he had done. I tend to believe that she headed home. Sick to her stomach, not knowing what to do next. I think she had to play it cool so it didn't look like to anyone that she knew what he did.

After Christopher killed Bella, he walked to the opposite battery than what he had put Cece in. I asked him why he put them in separate batteries. He said he wanted to get them as far away from Shanann as possible. It didn't make a lot of sense to me; however, nothing he did makes sense.

Cervi 319, this is where Bella and Cece met their doom. I've never been out there, but I've spoken to someone who has. He said he drove quite a distance to the middle of nowhere to get there. Even in the daytime, it's a desolate, creepy place. It is such a cold and horrible place for these little girls to be left. It would frighten anyone to be there at night, yet those little girls spent four nights out there alone; I know I repeat myself, but how could he do this? We know why that's been established, but how? It just makes no sense, and a person has to be the coldest of all monsters to do this.

There has always been a rumor about Christopher throwing up at the bottom of the battery stairs. When I asked him about that, he said it was Bella's vomit. I don't know if he is confused about that or what, but how could that have been Bella's vomit? So, this stands to create another theory that Bella was alive going up the battery stairs. I have to say it would not surprise me at all if she were alive while going up the stairs. I don't like to think about this as being true. However, he was clear when he said it was Bella's vomit. After he was finished, he told me he still felt so much anger. Anger was there because the girls spoiled everything by getting up after he thought he had killed them. Angry because Shanann just spoiled everything. That is not sensible thinking, for sure.

After he was all done and was pulling away from Cervi, he received a text from NK telling him to listen to the Metallica song "Batteries." Please google that song and tell me how appropriate the song fits what he did. I wish the police would have investigated this. It's just too much of a coincidence to be a coincidence. My belief again is that she was outside of his house after he killed his family.

CHAPTER 13

NK And Her Control

"Murder is unique in that it abolishes the party it injures, so that society must take the place of the victim and on his behalf demand atonement or grant forgiveness."

By: W.H. Auden

Another big false rumor is that NK has written Christopher in prison. I assure you she has never written him, not in code, by a different name, or any other way. I do not believe she ever wants to be associated with him again or caught having anything to do with him. I believe this because she is afraid. Afraid of being looked at again. I can see the authorities telling her to disappear and never come back. Whatever the reason, I can promise you 100% that NK has never written to him since he has been incarcerated.

So many things about NK need to be brought before the authorities and ask them why she is not investigated more thoroughly. If they have investigated her in a very deep way, then they need to be more forthcoming. However, I do not believe they have. They had their guy, and NK convinced them she knew nothing about his idea or reason to kill his wife.

One of the things I noticed in her interview with Law Enforcement is how she tried to make things that happened between her and Christopher seem so long ago when some of them had only been two days prior. If you will notice, she makes that comment several times in the interview. You would have thought they had their affair two or three years in the past.

She controlled the interview; the police hardly said anything, only asking a few questions during all the hours of her interview. I also believe she lied over and over to law enforcement. It was very suspicious why she deleted all of their messages to each other. If she had nothing to hide, why would she do that?

The fact that NK went to law enforcement before they came to her is just a ploy to look innocent. Law Enforcement considered her "forthcoming," but was it? Or was she just trying to get a jump on things to make herself look innocent? She was trying to pull an Amber Fry. They immediately considered her a protective witness. Why? From the beginning, she was considered someone who was only there to help. Before they were able to verify anything she told them, they were willing to tell her she was not a suspect.

NK told law enforcement she was so afraid that she could not sleep. Why would she be so afraid if she had nothing to do with what had happened? I have recalled the phone conversation they had on Sunday night, but when asked, NK could not come up with any real content. Christopher first told me they had phone sex, but later, when I asked him about it again, he changed his story. She seems again to take over the narrative of the conversation and lead law enforcement down a different path so she doesn't have to answer the question, which seems to work.

I have never understood why it was so important for Christopher to cover for NK. Even before he was asked, he wanted to make sure they knew she had nothing to do with the crime, even to the extent of going to prison for the rest of his life. Although I must make it clear, again, he did this: he killed his family with his own hands. He is in prison for the rest of his life, and in prison is where he belongs. Justice must be served, however, and I believe for justice to be completely served, NK has to be considered by law enforcement again as having something to do with what happened.

CHAPTER 14

The Truth Be Told

"I object to violence because when it appears to do good, the good is only temporary. The evil it does is permanent."

By: Gandhi

I don't understand why many people want to change the story to fit their beliefs. I sat in front of Christopher; I saw his eyes, evil eyes, as he talked about what he did. Whether it was his life with Shanann that he was so tired of, his family's dislike for Shanann, or if it was NK's influence, I tell you Christopher killed his family with his own hands. He did not have help in killing them. I do believe NK had some sort of mind control over him. Enough to tell him to get rid of Shanann. Again, I believe he took whatever NK was telling him and killed his family. I think she was horrified after she found out he had killed not only Shanann but his three children. I do not believe she ever meant for that to happen. Christopher is simple-minded but smart. I have already said he was very used to following whatever the women in his life told him to do.

Let's give thought to that; his mother was telling him about Shanann's attack on her because of nut-gate. She wanted him to do something to stop Shanann from what she believed were her many attacks on her. Shanann told him she was sick and tired of his mother's persistent disrespect for her authority over her children. Telling him she had come to the end of her rope with his mother, telling him to put a stop to it. NK told him she wanted him to get rid of Shanann, leave her, and stop meeting her many demands. She encouraged him as someone who could make his own decisions and not be ruled by the woman he was married to. I do not believe she ever had anything against his children.

We saw in the interrogation of Christopher how the FBI agent suggested something, and he picked that up as his narrative. He ran with it and carried that all through his sentencing and beyond. His mother believed it up until my book came out. Then, she turned against believing that he killed his family at all. Largely because of this woman I told you about in the above chapter.

NK is a strong woman, strong enough to try a much different approach to controlling Christopher. She had her eyes set on him; she wanted him, and she sat out to make sure she got him. Set him up for the perfect murder, *so he thought*. I believe she also controlled his mind by giving him the drinks that altered his thinking.

I believe he could not take the pressure he was under any longer. I believe he thought he hated Shanann. The five weeks he was without his family and with NK made him feel free again, reminding him of what it was like before he started to date Shanann. He had no responsibility and no one other than his mother to answer to. He wanted to be free of his baggage. NK convinced him life could be simpler. I believe it was freeing for him to think about all of them being gone.

One thing that is very common in all of the murderers I talk to is how narcissistic they are. They think they are smarter than everyone else. They hold many things in their minds and talk to no one about it. They are sinister and conniving, and they play out fantasies in their minds. Usually, they try to blame something or someone else for their actions.

When I sat with Christopher and talked with him, the look he gave me as he talked made me very uncomfortable. After spending hours with him, I would leave the prison wanting to vomit. I assure you that sitting with a family annihilator is very different than sitting with anyone else.

It's very sad for Shanann and the three children to have lost their lives. When I think about it, I can honestly cry for them. Beautiful souls were taken way before their time. God does not will this or ordain what happened to them, also, for Christopher, a young man only thirty-three at the time. He gave up his life forever on this earth and is spending the rest of his life with like-minded people. Having to look over his shoulder always because I assure you there are those in that prison that would love to take him out.

Following is a message I received from a dear friend who also writes to Christopher. She is a Christian mom who shares the Bible and tries to put light into his life. She has written to him for a couple of years after I gave her his address. She is a married mother with no romantic interest in him. Here is what she said about him.

Chris doesn't blame anyone. He has accepted where he is and knows he'll be there forever. Chris wants it left alone and people to stop trying to get him out. I agree that there are so many inconsistencies in the case, and I think there were other people involved, but either way, he knows he's there, and nothing will change that. He says he can't remember anyone else being there but doesn't understand the time frame or why her phone pinged near him. In his head, it's like a bad dream that he can't exactly put together, just pieces.

People can be cruel, and they don't always know the entirety of what comes with putting yourself out there like that. He's not a victim of his actions but faces those consequences daily and will for the rest of his life. I think that's why I pity people in that situation because there is no restoration, no help, and no form of reforming people. It's locking them up and throwing away the key, in a sense. Do I believe people who kill should live normal lives? No. But I think it should depend on the person, the offense, and the circumstances surrounding the situation. He ruthlessly blames his parents, and that's ruthless to me; they didn't make him do anything. He said his work phone and his personal phone pinged in different places. That's very weird, and Chris said he just doesn't remember anyone else being there, but he feels NK is into witchcraft and that she played a huge role in everything. I don't think Jim is innocent, either. Chris feels it's really weird that no one has spotted her in four years.

He said he wished he knew all the details just for his parent's sake. I think NK planned everything and may have assisted with some of the background things like disposal and preparation.

I feel confident that he killed Shanann and had the idea in his head, but when he knew she knew about the affair, he was scared of her and did it out of fear. Shanann was intimidating to him. She ruled that house and would probably beat the crap out of him if she knew he was cheating. She seemed like the I'll take everything you've got and make your life miserable type. I think she was a great mom and loved her family, but Chris was her little trophy husband, and he had expectations to be met. I think she belittled and silenced him a lot, and it caused resentment and anger in him that he couldn't voice. I don't know if you've ever done anything you were scared of your spouse to know, but it's a crippling feeling, and when you know, they know, and you're just waiting for an explosion, and you're walking on eggshells, and it's unbearable. I think that's what was going on, and he was guilty, egged on by NK, and scared of the consequences, so when he saw that there was no hope for him and ran out of excuses, he did it. I feel confident that he murdered Shanann, but the girls puzzle me because I don't know why he would keep them alive before leaving the house. Even if they did wake up, why wouldn't he just redo it at home? Unless someone else did it the first time, and it was an amateur, he was again egged on.

My daughter is the same age as Bella and is no dummy. She knows what death is. She knows you can't breathe when blankets are on your head, and if she walked in on something like that, she is old enough to understand and tell what happened. So I feel like if she caught him, he would panic. I don't think it was *his* plan. I think if he did it, it was a last resort. But a part of me thinks he's too much of a wimp to do that to his girls.

I truly feel like even if NK or Jim did it, he'd take it to his grave because he can't prove it, and he knows he's there for life, so why mess up theirs at this point? I think that's how he thinks. I think he was so scared, and the thought was put in his mind by NK. He, to this day, can't remember that 111-minute phone call. Something had to be going on in his soul, as in demon possession, or he was given some type of mind-altering drug, drink, etc. It was something. A normal dad who takes kids to birthday parties, reads stories, makes lunches, and plays on the floor with his kids doesn't do something like that without some explanation. There is no history of violence or weird behavior. I think that's what his parents want to know. How does that happen so suddenly?

He comments how he wishes he'd gone to the Rockies game; something changed that whole situation that night. He was shy and socially awkward. NK was possessive and controlling in her own way. He didn't really know her as a person. Their relationship was sex only. She did her controlling with her female organs. NK used the fact that men are very sexual to her advantage. He definitely had a lust issue at that point. You'd be surprised what people have access to these days. It's hard not to come in contact with perversion.

I think they did satanic rituals and crap. No matter what my husband could do to me, I would never kill someone; that's why I believe it's satanic. It has to be. From what I've seen, they stopped investigating her when he pled guilty to all of it. I'm not saying he's not a liar, but I listen to holes in his stories, and lately, I feel like he just wants peace. He wants people to stop making it a spectacle because he knows it continually hurts people.

CHAPTER 15

Christopher's Forever Home

"We are so accustomed to disguising ourselves to others that in the end, we become disguised to ourselves."

By: Francois de la Rochefoucauld

So where is Christopher now? What is he doing? He works in the prison hospital. He shares the Bible and his religion with sometimes dying inmates. He has a girlfriend, Lexie. She contacted me one day and asked for my opinion. However, the women that he becomes fond of seem to fall for his boyish charm and end up feeling he was wronged. They don't take my advice. However, she seems like a nice person, and she does recognize he has a sexual addiction, but I think she feels like he really loves her. When I asked him about her, I thought he was denying he knew her, and I told her he said he didn't know her. She became very angry with me and cut me off. I read his message wrong and realized he was saying yes, he did know her. However, he never admitted that he loved her. He probably just gave her the same lines he gives to many women who write to him. Interesting, though, is how much she looks like Shanann. Do I believe God has forgiven him for what he has done? If, with a true heart, he wants forgiveness, then yes, I believe God has forgiven him. However, he still has consequences, and consequences can be a bitch.

He is trying to find some purpose in where he is now, but people do not really want to talk about that. He's done a lot of terrible things, but I'm a believer that God can use him where he is now to help others and do some good. I don't think any of us can relate to the dark life prison would be. You live in a very small place; you are told what to do and what not to do. No one loves you. No one celebrates your birthday or your accomplishments. You don't get to enjoy your family, Christmas, or any holiday. You will not be allowed to bury your parents when they pass or sit with them when they are very ill. All of your rights have been taken. Most of all, you have no human touch. No one gives you a hug, or a kiss, or touches you at all. I believe this is why so many inmates turn to sex with another man—because they need human touch. We are made for that. Of course, this is the way it should be when you choose to murder your wife and three children.

A person has to work hard in prison to change who they are. They don't receive any help or guidance. My friend went on to say that the devil is a roaring lion seeking whom he can devour. He looks for easy targets, people with money, lust, or pride problems. He prowls on the weak, and when he gets you, he will take you farther than you ever want to go. We have an advocate with the Father who will help those who want to be helped. Forgiveness is available, but there will always be consequences for your actions, good and bad.

He still has his three meals a day and all he wants from the commissary. He receives many letters every day. A lot of them have money in them—$10.00 to $20.00, some more. People who send him money also are feeding his ego. He is made to feel important; I wonder if it makes him somehow delusional about whether he killed his family. These things are all he has to pull from. Possibly all he has to keep from losing his sanity. Because, at times, he says he can't clearly remember what happened. I don't believe he can't remember. However, I do believe there are things he remembers that he will not share with anyone. He commented once that there is no need to talk about NK or Jim or their part in anything, so why ruin their lives, too?

Another thing I have a problem with is how you say you serve Christ but then spread lies about applying for an appeal. Christopher is not going to appeal his case. I know for a fact, and he knows that. I'm unsure if it's him or if his family tries to keep this case going.

I know that the YouTuber Dave knows nothing about the case. Christopher has never talked to or written to him and knows nothing about him beyond what his parents tell him. He has tried to get them to stop being friends with Dave and not to believe what he says. Don't be fooled by this person; he is just doing this for money, no other reason.

The families of both Shanann and Christopher have no peace in their lives. Whether it's because someone is always trying to steer people or because they are being hassled by the media or the public, this is their business, and I guess his family would do almost anything to get him freed from prison. However, Christopher will never be free again in this life. It makes one sad to think he will never be able to go to his parent's funeral or be with a loved one when they are sick.

But Christopher took the lives of innocent, precious children and the life of an unsuspecting wife, all who loved and trusted him with everything. People, even the family of Shanann and Christopher, want to believe that NK is to blame. She was a Conduit for his evilness. Had it not been NK, it would have been someone or something else. This monster lived(s) inside of him and probably has for many years. I believe a murderer is born in most situations, and the bad things around them nourish the evil inside of them. Who knew when he was ten years old, he had this living inside of him? I believe he knew and has always known.

When NK came along and "swept him off his feet," who knew she would try to do mind control over him? Yet I believe that is exactly what happened. I believe it was easy, and through it, the monster was released. Again, I believe it was an affair for her, possibly a game, but it turned deadly. Very deadly. I think she was trying out her skills in this business she was trying to run. Maybe she did not realize the danger of what she was doing because she was unskilled. Whatever it was that happened, I do believe his killing of his family was a complete and utter surprise for her.

NK was having an affair with a married man. That was horrible, but Shanann would have survived that. Bella and Cece would have survived it. If every woman who had an affair with a married man had to face what NK has faced, our world would be very confusing and awful. And let's remember, she only can be blamed for 50% of the affair.

CHAPTER 16

The Dark Calling

"Whoever undertakes to set himself up as judge in the field of truth and knowledge is shipwrecked by the laughter of the gods."

Never could I have guessed what lay ahead for me when I set out to write this book. On August 14, 2018, early morning, I stood in front of the television screen and watched Christopher as he smirked out, "I just want my family back. Bella, Cece, Shanann, please come home". Knowing exactly where they were, he was barely able to hold back his full-on smile. Standing there watching him, I felt something nudge me. I had always wanted to write a book; I always knew someday I would. That voice inside of me felt like a calling. I told my husband this guy is as guilty as he could be. I'm going to contact him and get the real story from him and write a book about it. My husband looked at me, grinned (always supportive), and said ok, you can do that. I knew he was appeasing me; he did not believe it would ever happen. I stayed glued to the case, finding out and watching everything I possibly could about the case.

Then, after sentencing and moving him to Wisconsin, I set out to write to him. I wrote to him right after he was sent to Wisconsin but didn't hear back from him. I felt sure he never received my letter so I wrote another one. I waited, but still nothing. Then I wrote to him a third time, and within a few days he wrote back.

My husband and I had been out for dinner, and when we came home, he walked to the mailbox. He came running back, saying, "You got a letter from a prison in Wisconsin! I didn't know you wrote this guy! He said here's the letter but don't open it until I get in the house. He was bringing garbage cans in. He was so funny because he was shocked I wrote Christopher but even more shocked that he wrote me back.

We opened the letter together, and I read it out loud. Christopher told me he was sorry that he was just now writing me back. He wrote that "God" told him to write me back and write a book with me. I was very clear from day one with Christopher that this was not a love letter but an attempt to tell the truth about his story. He said he wanted to clear Shanann's name because he had left it that she had killed the girls. He went on to say God had forgiven him and thanked me for telling him that God could still use him. I meant that. He was in a place of kindred hearts, and I know that God can use anyone to achieve whatever his purpose—even Christopher, who had killed his entire family. Just about a week later, while at work one day, I received a phone call from Cindy Watts, Christopher's mother. She said Christopher had asked her to call me and tell me he wrote me back and was sorry he hadn't written sooner. She said he wanted to talk to me as soon as we could. She gave me the information I needed to know to set up the account for him to call me.

Cindy also said she was mailing the form for me to fill out to be approved to visit Christopher at the prison. She mailed that form along with several pictures she wanted me to have. Her letter stated that I should use the pictures in the book or any way I saw fit.

About one week before I could see Christopher at the prison, the FBI came to see him. They wanted the full story (of course). He had never told the truth about what happened. He told me he was later angry they just showed up at the prison without notice.

As we know, he gave the FBI many details, but not all of the details. Within the next two weeks, I made plans to see him. The prison had ok'd me for a visit. My heart sank into my stomach with the news, "You've been approved to come see Christopher Watts." Not that I looked at him as a celebrity, but I could hardly believe I was going to sit face-to-face with this man. My husband and I made plans to travel to Wisconsin the following weekend. The prison was about a four-hour drive from where I live. We left on a Saturday morning early so we could be there by the time visiting hours began at 3:00 p.m. I had five hours to spend with him on the first day and about three hours on Sunday. I cannot tell you how nervous I was. Nervous sickness is a better description. My husband walked into the prison with me until I got through the security. He then waited in the general area until I was finished. I remember I walked through about seven security doors before I got to the area of visitation.

The first time I visited Christopher, he was in what they call "protective custody." Meaning he was in a cell for twenty-three hours a day. He could not be moved from place to place without them shutting down the entire hallway, which meant every prisoner had to go back to their cell, and the cells were locked; this would upset the prisoners, and I could hear them yelling (at the time, not knowing what they were yelling about) this made Christopher very nervous. When they brought him into the room to talk with me, I could tell he was very nervous. The first time we met was through a glass divider, and we talked on the prison telephone. I felt sorry for him at the time because he was shackled and cuffed to the table. We talked for five hours that first day. Three hours the next day. After that, there were occasional visits and almost daily phone calls. Sometimes, more than one call a day. Christopher was well aware of the book and what was in it. Never did I misguide him about anything, regardless of the rumors.

Please join my Facebook group at *Tea Time And True Crime* with author Cheryln Cadle.

EPILOGUE

Hope To Talk With You Later

"In a time of universal deceit, telling the truth is a revolutionary act."

By: George Orwell

Again, I want to say the narrative in this book is my opinion, and they do not reflect the opinions of others; this is my theory, and I am not claiming this to be what happened. It's just my opinion from what I believe through my research what has happened in this case. I keep saying this is the last time I will write about Christopher, and I do hope I won't be writing about him again. I felt everyone needed and would want a true update on what was going on. I'm not sure why he is so interesting to people, but I do feel many just want justice for Shanann and her babies. Justice that can't be found until the authorities investigate NK. For the love of all things good and truthful, we need the authorities to investigate. Everyone deserves to know she was investigated thoroughly; I believe that has not been done. I believe she was in that house many more times than she has admitted, has slept at his house, and wanted Shanann's life. I believe she tried to use mind control over him, and that was not hard to do with his simple mind.

As for me, I will continue with my life and continue to write about true crime and get information about their crimes and put it into a book form. It's what I am passionate about and what I love to do. None of us enjoy that people kill their family members or innocent people, but since they do, I think it helps to bring the victim's voices to the forefront. So people know who they were and that they deserve to be remembered. They deserve justice. So, I usually write about the unknown, the innocent, and the unfortunate. Most of them meet a violent and horrible end.

I've been married now for fifty-one years. I have three children I am very proud of—all very decent citizens and people with very high integrity. I have twelve grandchildren and two great-grandchildren. I love my precious Dylan, my eighteen-year-old grandson. We have three little Morkies that are spoiled more than I can say. I love animals and cannot stand for any animal to be abused. My life is mostly peaceful and happy. I put God first in my life, and I try to live the most decent life I can. I love people, and I want to always be kind. I have been accused of many things that are not true. People are cruel and don't care how they treat others. I have learned, though, that you will reap what you sow. Therefore, it is all in God's hands.

I have been to many places across the United States, and people have recognized me and come up and talk to me. I love that, so if I'm ever in your area and you recognize me, please come and say hello. I guess I just want people to know my heart is to try and find the truth in these cases and write the truth for those who are seeking answers in these cases. My intent is never to hurt anyone. Although negative things may be said, they are truthful, and unfortunately, in these cases, there are many negative things that have to be said.

For the price of a fast-food meal, you can buy one of my books. I hope you will join me in the future to learn about more of these horrible crimes. I'm always on a quest to learn as much as I can about these people who commit such awful acts, how they think, and how their minds work.

I love my Facebook group and how they enjoy digging for answers. Honestly, you are what has kept me going; you have encouraged me to stick with the truth and tell it. I thank and love you all so much! I want to thank my son Michael, who has been the biggest help you can imagine. He took a college-level course to help me proofread, and this has given my book a great look. He has encouraged me so much, and I love and appreciate him.

To Brandi! I thank you for all you do to help with the Facebook group. You are always watching out for me and standing up for me whenever necessary.

To Gina, thank you for your hard work helping with the Facebook group. I feel our group has the utmost integrity and tries not to have any drama.

To my husband, I thank you. Who is always supportive and encourages me to just keep writing. He knows my heart and knows my passions. He knows I'm here to tell you the truth.

If you are reading this, then I thank you for your support. It's greatly appreciated.

I want to take a moment to list my books. Always on Amazon, or you can order straight from me. After the books have been out for a while, you can purchase them in-store. I love signing and mailing you my books.

The Murders of Christopher Watts
Love Must Cry
Suffer the Little Children
The Many Faces of Christopher Watts

I have another book coming soon; there will be fifteen more cases of people who have been murdered. I find these stories very intriguing. I hope you do, too.

Love, Cheryln

THE END